NUCLEAR POWER AND NON-PROLIFERATION

NUCLEAR POWER AND NON-PROLIFERATION

Air Commodore
Jasjit Singh
AVSM VrC VM IAF (Retd)
(Editor)

Knowledge World

in association with

Centre for Strategic & International Studies

The Centre for Strategic & International Studies is an independent, non-profit, academic reseach institution established in 2002 under a registered trust to undertake and promote policy-related research, study and discussion on the trends and developments in international relations and national security interests and issues in a comprehensive and inclusive framework. Its publications seek to expand and deepen the understanding of strategic and foreign policy issues without necessarily reflecting the views of any institution or individuals except those of the author.

Jasjit Singh
Director
Centre for Strategic & International Studies
No. 1, Vasant Enclave
New Delhi-110057

Telefax: (91-11) 5166.2712 and 2713
E-mail: csis_india@yahoo.co.in

Knowledge World
5A/4A Ansari Road, Daryaganj, New Delhi 110002

Published in India by Knowledge World

ISBN: 81-87966-31-9

Typeset and Printed by Hardev Printers, Nirankari Colony, Delhi-110009.
Published by Kalpana Shukla, Knowledge World, 5A/4A Ansari Road, Daryaganj, New Delhi-110002.

Contents

Atoms for Peace and Prosperity: An Introductory Essay

*Jasjit Singh**

> In the last forty years we have seen nuclear energy take its place as a major source of electricity worldwide, on both economic and resource strategy grounds. Today the question of global warming focuses attention on the extent to which nuclear energy offsets it, and may increasingly do so in the future.
>
> — Ian Hore-Lacy*

December 2003 marked the fiftieth anniversary of President Dwight D. Eisenhower's "Atoms for Peace" speech to the United Nations General Assembly. Eisenhower was a visionary in this regards since at that time, nuclear power was not yet a reality in the lives of people. At the same time, the very concept of "Atoms for Peace" emphasised the potential of nuclear technology for peaceful purposes, from medicine to electricity. This speech had provided the impetus for the formation of the US commercial nuclear industry with an incredible growth in civilian nuclear energy production during the next two decades, and now it provides 20 per cent of total US electricity output. But more important, "Atoms for Peace" led directly to the establishment of the International Atomic Energy Agency (IAEA) to promote the development and sharing of nuclear science and technology for peaceful purposes. President Eisenhower, in his December 1953 address to the UN General Assembly at the time of the creation of the IAEA, stated:

---

* Jasjit Singh is Director, Centre for Strategic & International Studies, New Delhi.

* Ian Hore-Lacy, "The Future of Nuclear Energy," paper presented at the Royal College of Physicians Conference, Adelaide, May 4, 2000.

> The most important responsibility of this atomic energy agency would be to devise methods whereby this fissionable material would be allocated to serve the needs of mankind. Experts would be mobilised to apply atomic energy to the needs of agriculture, medicine, and other peaceful uses. *A special purpose would be to provide abundant electrical energy in the power-starved areas of the world*" (emphasis added).

What was left unstated in the statement about "power-starved" regions of the world was that these regions were also mostly poor and starving regions of the world. To many such regions, peace meant the hope of prosperity some day, while the immediate task was the need to stay alive, try and get rid of perennial debilitating poverty, hunger and disease. India's case is symptomatic although it was far more developed than most developing countries. Less than a decade before Eisenhower's "Atoms for Peace" proposal, the Great Bengal Famine in only one province of pre-partition India under the rule of the British Raj in India had killed 3.5 million people, with perhaps 15-odd million suffering from under-nourishment. It would take India two decades after independence in 1947 to craft the Green Revolution and attain self-sufficiency in foodgrains. A significant factor in this process comprised the additions to electricity availability for agricultural purposes within the larger eight-fold increase in the generation capacity in the country during the two decades after 1950.

At the same time, deindustrialisation of India for two centuries before independence had left a deep backwardness, making widespread poverty that much more difficult to roll back. Even three years after India became independent, the country had an installed capacity of a mere 2.3 MW of electricity. This had reached a figure of around 125 MW by 2003 (up four times since 1981), but without being able to meet current needs of industry, agriculture and domestic consumption, leave alone hold out the promise of power shortages being removed any time soon. But it is also clear that more abundant electric power would be needed for poverty elimination and moving a population of a billion plus towards a better quality of life and prosperity. For India, therefore, Eisenhower's concept has greater meaning if it is seen as *"Atoms for Peace and Prosperity."*

It also needs to be noted that while India has large reserves of coal (mostly of the variety that could blow a hole in the ozone layers if used more extensively), it has been an energy-deficient country from the time it became independent. Its future socio-economic development and well-being depend greatly on the access to energy resources. In turn, national security requires a satisfactory level of energy security that meets future needs. Diversification of the source of energy and type of energy, hence, is an essential strategy for that security, especially when it is recognised that oil and natural gas are mostly located in politically tension-filled areas. This is not the place to go into the details of India's energy security challenges and possible responses, except to emphasise that if India has to eliminate poverty and ensure faster human development of its large population which continues to grow, greater access to nuclear power is a critical necessity.

It is in this context that we have to assess the imperatives of nuclear power and the risks of nuclear proliferation. The problem would be simplified if the international community were to move robustly toward global nuclear disarmament so that nuclear technology can be used exclusively for peaceful purposes. Unfortunately, the expectations that after the end of Cold War (which had driven the nuclear arms race), nuclear disarmament would start to receive higher priority have been belied by events of the past decade. But what is needed under the circumstances is an approach that tries to reconcile the goals of nuclear technology for peaceful purposes and those of nuclear non-proliferation. It is with this aim that the Centre for Strategic and International Studies, New Delhi, organised a national seminar in May 2004 to look at the issues involved in this process. This volume includes the papers presented at this seminar and other studies from the centre.

Nuclear Non-Proliferation

It is a travesty of historical logic of the IAEA that it has come to signify more an agency to control and deny nuclear technology for peaceful purposes in the name of nuclear non-proliferation than serve the purpose for which it was established in spite of its heads trying to argue for promoting nuclear power. The director general of the IAEA is more often referred to as the "chief UN inspector" for non-proliferation rather than as the head of the international agency to provide abundant nuclear technology for peaceful purposes. Even the infamous nuclear Non-Proliferation Treaty (NPT) which seeks to limit the possession of nuclear weapons with the five permanent members of the UN Security Council, affirms in (Article IV) to the "inalienable right of all Parties to the Treaty to develop research, production and use of nuclear energy for peaceful purposes without discrimination…" The Article goes on to commit all parties to "cooperate in contributing alone or together with other (non-NPT member) States or international organisations to the further development of the applications of nuclear energy for peaceful purposes…with due consideration for the needs of the developing areas of the world." But the concerns about the spread of nuclear weapons led to the original purpose of promotion of nuclear energy for peaceful purposes to be overtaken by non-proliferation agendas. During the 1990s, it reached a new crescendo with a series of non-proliferation measures brought into vogue which the IAEA is expected to monitor. Many of these, like the Nuclear Suppliers Group (NSG) Guidelines, are ad hoc creations to deny nuclear technology and materials to even non-nuclear weapon states members of the NPT.

There can be no doubt that nuclear proliferation poses one of the most serious risks to international peace and security. Unfortunately, the ad hoc approach to implementing non-proliferation has harmed both non-proliferation as well as cooperation for use of nuclear energy for peaceful purposes. The case of North Korea, the ninth nuclear weapon state, is symptomatic.

At the same time, the example of a number of NPT member states acquiring nuclear weapons technology and material from Pakistan's nuclear bazaar proves the limitations and inadequacy of the non-proliferation regimes, in principle as well as in practice. Non-proliferation might have been more successful if more innovative approaches had been adopted instead of the linear paradigm that became the favourite of the nuclear weapon states. The end result has been that a major war (followed by more than a year of continuing armed conflict) was waged in Iraq only to discover that there were no nuclear weapons or a programme at least after 1993 in the country, as indeed was being maintained by the UN/IAEA inspectors.

It is in this milieu that India became a target as well as the victim of ill-advised nuclear non-proliferation, from national policies of some states as well as the larger global agenda. India was one of the first states to start research and development of a nuclear programme for peaceful purposes. With the progressive development of indigenous nuclear science and technology, it could, of course, have acquired nuclear weapons a long time ago. But it opted to search for a solution to its security dilemma of an increasingly nuclearised environment by pressing for universal nuclear disarmament. In fact, as the prospects for disarmament receded and the non-proliferation regime based on technology denial even for normal developmental purposes was brought within its ambit under the rubric of "dual-technology," it saw no option but to seek "time-bound" nuclear disarmament as the means of increasing the political diplomatic pressure almost in step with the rise of the non-proliferation pressures and the *mantra* of "cap, reduce and eliminate" nuclear capabilities of India.

But one central factor remained constant through the decades: India would not indulge in supporting or in any way assisting in any nuclear proliferation for love of God or money, unlike our worthy neighbour who did it for both. There were many people in our country who expected that such responsible conduct itself should have led to suitable recognition and better cooperation from the dominant powers in India's efforts to expand the use of nuclear technology for peaceful purposes. But in what is claimed to be a pragmatic world, pragmatism seems to have only rewarded the proliferators, rather than the responsible states. The United States turning a blind eye to Pakistan's nuclear programme, and providing massive military-economic aid to obtain its concurrence for being a "frontline state" in Afghanistan in 1981 against the Soviet Union was an example.[1] Pakistan also obtained assistance for its clandestine nuclear weapons programme from China on whose territory it actually tested the first nuclear device in 1983, believed to be based on an earlier Chinese nuclear weapon design.[2] And now once again its papering over of Islamabad's nuclear proliferation to a large number of countries where acquisition of such capabilities directly impinged negatively on the strategic and security interests of the United States and its traditional allies, and providing Pakistan with the status and substance of a major non-North Atlantic Treaty Organisation (NATO) ally and pumping in economic and military aid in return for its willingness to be a "frontline state" against terrorism (that it had nurtured) is another case.

It is not as if the IAEA has not lived up to its mandate. In fact, the IAEA has tried hard to encourage the expansion of safe and efficient use of nuclear technology for peaceful purposes. But the non-proliferation regimes and pressures are crafted outside the IAEA which is then expected to monitor the rules for implementation. And, hence, the dubious title of "watchdog" given to the agency and its head. Among its innumerable efforts to promote nuclear power, the resolution passed by its General Conference is valuable in indicating the commitment and policy of the IAEA:

> The International Atomic Energy Agency, considering...the peaceful use of nuclear energy will contribute to the well-being and help enrich the quality of life of peoples of the world...conscious of the great potential of nuclear power for meeting energy requirements of many countries and the need to protect the environment and recognising that many countries consider nuclear power, being a

climatically benign source of energy, to be an eligible option under the Clean Development Mechanism of the Kyoto Protocol...requests the Director General to pursue...efforts to strengthen the technical cooperation activities of the Agency...aimed at improving the scientific, technological and regulatory capabilities of developing countries...by continuing to assist them in their.

(a) peaceful applications of atomic energy and nuclear techniques in the fields of *inter alia* food and agriculture, human health, industry, water resource management, environment; and

(b) nuclear energy production for those states pursuing it as a component of their energy mix in the 21st century.[3]

Revival of Nuclear Power

It is against this background that we need to look at the phenomenon of revival of nuclear power worldwide during the past few years. It is also clear that this revival is not transient and would actually pick up greater momentum in the coming decades. The central reason for this revival is that nuclear power is not only the most economical source of electricity, but is crucial for sustainable development. This revival is led by the United States itself where 20 per cent of the country's electricity comes from nuclear energy. The accident at Chernobyl in 1986, even more than the earlier accident in 1979 at the Three Mile Island facility in the USA, had certainly created a strong public opinion wave against nuclear power which only got reinforced by the nuclear non-proliferation drive, especially after the end of the Cold War and hence the criticism was more vocal in the West. But two facts related to Chernobyl also need to be noted. One was that this accident took place in the former Soviet space while the Cold War was still on. Second, the design of the reactor was of an earlier period when safety measures like double-containment chambers had not come into vogue.

It may be recalled that the United States had stopped constructing new nuclear power plants nearly two decades ago and even the additional demand of electricity with population growth at the minimal, was being met by conservation methods and technologies.

But the prospects of oil shortages and the likelihood of global oil production peaking around 2030 AD with little prospect of any recovery from the ensuing decline after that have made the US and other countries of the Organisation of Economic Cooperation and Development (OECD) rethink their energy policies, with a renewed emphasis on nuclear energy, with the possible exception of Germany. The United States relies on oil mainly for transportation, meeting its other needs of industry, etc. by electricity generated by nuclear power plants and coal-fired facilities. Even then, its imports of oil have been increasing and are expected to jump to 70 per cent of the consumption in a couple of years.

It is, therefore, not surprising that President Bush had called on Congress last year to support nuclear energy stating that "Congress should promote research into the next generation of nuclear plants and encourage investment in existing nuclear plants to expand a clean and unlimited source of energy."[4] In a bipartisan resolution supporting nuclear energy, introduced in the US House of Representatives on June 3, 2004, Congress "supports the increased use of nuclear power and the construction and development of new and improved nuclear generating power plants as a means of contributing to national energy independence and maintaining a clean environment."[5]

India's Energy Needs

A number of factors started to impinge heavily on the energy scenario of the country since the early 1960s. Population growth rate increased significantly, increasing the requirement of energy. Unlike the US and most developed industrialised countries, rising population naturally demanded more energy even if the level of industrialisation remained generally stagnant. Secondly, the spread of industrialisation and mechanised transportation started to increase the demand for energy, especially oil which provides the fuel for the bulk of transportation and, therefore, a major segment of economic activity. Economic growth since the 1990s has had a special impact on energy demand, shifting it to high gear. While successive oil shocks had a serious deleterious impact on our economy, it was generally assumed that we can contain the fall-out and there would be no long-term negative implication of energy dependency on foreign sources. However, this perception is no longer valid in view of the changed circumstances.

The Gulf crisis and war of 1990-91 resulted in imposing a direct cost of Rs. 4,000 crore (equal to 26 per cent of that year's defence budget) on the economy. Geopolitics of energy started to alter in significant ways ranging from the war in Afghanistan in the 1980s, to control of Central Asian oil and natural gas, to the rising demands of energy in China and India. More important, concerns about climate change and environmental security began to influence politics and policy worldwide.

China became a net importer of energy after 1992 and set about putting in place major long-term plans to ensure its energy security in the coming decades. This was based on exercising multiple choices for sources of energy: oil and natural gas pipelines for Central Asia, greater control over the South China Sea, rapid build-up of the nuclear energy base (which incidentally was virtually absent at the end of the 1980s although it had built nuclear weapons by 1964!), construction of high-value, environmentally questionable hydroelectric mega-projects like the "Three Gorges" dam system, etc. China already has nine reactors with a combined capacity of 6,500 MW. Nuclear power forms a part of a long-term plan which aims to invest $30 billion to raise China's nuclear capacity to almost 40,000 MW by 2020.[6] Compared to this programme, India, which currently has 14 reactors with an installed capacity of nearly 2,500 MW, plans to acquire 20,000 MW of nuclear power capacity by 2020 in spite of having a far more well-established indigenous nuclear science and technology programme, especially for peaceful purposes. The rapidly increasing gap between the two countries' nuclear programmes is essentially due to the fact that China is not subject to any of the non-proliferation restrictions and sanctions although it has been believed to have been responsible for a great deal of nuclear proliferation activities.[7]

India's consumption of energy started to rise rapidly since the early 1990s. Compared to the scene at the end of the 1980s when one-third of oil was being imported and two-thirds of the demand was being met from indigenous production, the paradigm had reversed by the end of the 1990s. By that time, a mere one-third of the requirement of crude oil was being produced within the country and two-thirds of the consumption was being met from imports. At the present rate of economic growth, we would be importing around 85 per cent or more of our crude oil requirements by the end of this decade. The picture for natural gas is not very different, and our imports could touch over 80 per cent of the total consumption by the end of another decade.

In India, energy security is likely to be one of the biggest challenges to Indian policy-making in the coming decades since this, perhaps, more than any other single factor, would influence the pace of human development. India is at the stage of rising prosperity even though this is limited to only a comparatively small segment of society. But historically, revolutions occur at periods of growing prosperity, and not during periods of widespread poverty and/or during widespread prosperity. The reason is simple: disparities and perceptions of inequities generate a sense of relative deprivation which tends to provide incentives for resort to violence to restore the balance of equity. Others resort to violence to gain advantage in the struggle for greater prosperity. In recent years, the problem has been aggravated by the information revolution which has made people far more aware of what is possible in terms of the quality of life that might exist, while reality lags behind. Narrowing the increasing gap between expectations and satisfaction demands a sustained economic growth and expanded employment opportunities. Without access to sufficient energy resources at affordable costs, this goal may be difficult if not impossible to achieve within a desirable time-frame.

Looking at the future of oil and natural gas demand and consumption it is clear that India's import dependency would continue to rise markedly in the coming decade and beyond. But the greater challenge that must be addressed concurrently is that of dependency giving rise of vulnerability. This in itself requires that dependency on external sources be minimised to the extent possible, while diversification of sources of supply is ensured.

Energy security for the future, therefore, requires a coherent long-term policy that takes into account the geopolitical factors as well as techno-economic imperatives. This demands that we look at nuclear power far more seriously for our energy needs than perhaps has been done so far. But the two main handicaps to faster growth of nuclear energy in India are: (i) the nuclear non-proliferation regime; and (ii) public perceptions and concerns about the risks and costs of nuclear power being high, often driven by either lack of knowledge or over-emphasised by the non-proliferation campaigns.

Reconciling Nuclear Power and Non-Proliferation

The greatest handicap to a more robust approach to India's nuclear power growth emanates from the nuclear non-proliferation issues and policies of dominant powers. The application of most of them to India was aimed at stopping India from acquiring a nuclear weapon capability. India's own security interests would be better served if the world moved to universally abolish nuclear weapons. But in the absence of nuclear disarmament, India had no other option but to stay outside the legal commitment to the NPT since it would leave India undefended against nuclear weapon threats.[8] Keeping the nuclear option while working for nuclear disarmament, therefore, had become the central goal of strategic and diplomatic policy. The cost, of course, was the sanctions and effects of technology denial regimes balanced by greater indigenous technology development, making the Indian nuclear programme self-sufficient in terms of its peaceful applications as well in terms of weapons. And, hence, the sanctions have had less effect on the nuclear policies and programmes.[9]

But in a curiously ironic way, the primary impact of non-proliferation regimes has been to slow down India's nuclear power programme, thus, jeopardising its human and developmental security without in any way being able to slow (leave alone stop) the weapons programme!

Nearly six theoretically possible ways of reconciling global nuclear non-proliferation goals with India's need for nuclear power can be identified. These are briefly outlined in the following paragraphs, not necessarily in the order of feasibility or any preference. It may be that some of them or parts may have to be pursued concurrently. But before we try and outline these measures, it would be good to note some immutable issues. The first is that the NPT is not going to get unravelled or amended to accommodate India regardless of the advantage Washington sees in supporting Indian interests. We have certainly been highly critical of the NPT over the years. India cannot sign the NPT: I remember having told the US Secretary of Defence William Perry in January 1995, not so much because of domestic politics or the moral aspect of its discriminatory nature, but because we can become members only as a "non-nuclear weapon state" and this would jeopardise our short and long-term security interests in relation to potential nuclear weapons threat and coercion. We, therefore, have to seek accommodation within the existing NPT regime although with a certain amount of adjustment, especially in areas where ad hoc regimes rather than legally binding treaties and laws operate. Secondly, acceptance of any reconciliation measures would have to be acceptable to the majority of the non-nuclear weapon countries, with or without US diplomatic support.

Strobe Talbot in his recent book talks about the need to reconcile US (and the international community's) non-proliferation goals with Indian interests to say that "a set of agreements is imaginable that would stop short of granting India and Pakistan equal status with the five 'nuclear haves' in the eyes of the NPT. Rather than expanding the club to seven, there could be, in effect a '5+2' arrangement, whereby India and Pakistan would earn a degree of leniency in exchange for their yielding to international arms control measures and non-proliferation safeguards. They would be treated as NPT outliers rather than outlaws."[10] India, of course, could accept any measure only if it is compatible with its core security interests. But the important point is that while taking care of its security against nuclear threat and coercion, it also must balance this with the needs of economic and energy security for the future to enable adequate emphasis to be placed on human development. Unfortunately, such reconciliation has never really been discussed even at the non-governmental levels between India and the United States and other dominant powers.

The principles of what Strobe Talbot has hinted at could be served largely by adding a protocol to the NPT signed by India (and Pakistan) which would contain the key provisions of non-proliferation commitments in the NPT similar to (not necessarily the same as) those applicable to the five acknowledged nuclear weapon states. The immediate reaction to such an idea may be to discard it without further examination since it appears as rewarding the two NPT "holdouts." But if the aim is to ensure that India and Pakistan are brought into the non-proliferation fold, then they would have to be (a) accorded certain incentives to do so without trying to put them on a slippery slope to denuclearisation; and (b) bind them in legal and normative obligations for non-proliferation. By a sheer coincidence, this approach had been proposed many years ago by me and also by Abdul Sattar, a former foreign minister of Pakistan in a different forum and at different times without any mutual consultations. But given the absence of any willingness to look at goals other than getting India to sign the NPT as a non-nuclear weapon state, these received no attention at that time.

The protocol approach would have the advantage of serving the interests of sustaining the non-proliferation regime, especially the NPT, based on the ground realities. While India has acquired a compulsive opposition to the NPT, the prospects of progressively being treated as a normal state should help to accept the concept. The international community, on the other hand, would be able to ensure that nuclear non-proliferation is brought under a universal regime with all its moral, legal and political strength. Hypothetically, if such a regime had been in place earlier, the massive proliferation from Pakistan would not have taken place without inviting strong punitive measures which would have had the broadest support.

The other approach would be a bit-by-bit tinkering process which would slowly move toward mutually agreed arrangements like export controls by India and Pakistan in return for some relaxation of access to "dual-technology" commerce and nuclear power. The steps under the Next Steps for Strategic Partnership (NSSP) between the United States and India are predicated on this approach. The assumption is that India would meanwhile exercise due "restraint" in its strategic policy. This is a pragmatic approach on both sides except that it risks reversal at any time, depending upon factors possibly totally unconnected with the important issues involved in reconciliation of nuclear proliferation with the ground realities. India, of course, has no fundamental problem with either instituting export controls and/or exercising nuclear-missile restraint. Both these are stated objectives of Indian interests and policy. India has had a far better record (without any legal commitments) of non-proliferation than either the nuclear weapon states or other members of the NPT and its accompanying regimes. India has had no difficulty in accepting international safeguards on facilities and installations that produce electricity, especially with assistance from abroad. In fact, in had placed the Tarapur reactor voluntarily under IAEA safeguards after the initial 30-year agreement had expired in 1993. The two nuclear power plants being built with Russian assistance at Kudankulam would also be under international safeguards. Similar principles would naturally be applicable to any future supplies of equipment and plants.

Washington may want to see India's nuclear posture remain restrained and possibly give up the concept of triad. Since India has adopted a doctrine and strategy of "no-first-use," restraint becomes inbuilt if it has to be translated into strategy and posture as the most cost-effective solution to defence against a nuclear threat.[11] What Washington should be interested in is whether India would go in for intercontinental ballistic missiles to target the United States? But that would depend upon the nature of Indo-US relations in the coming decades and Indian perceptions of the political-strategic necessity to target the US homeland. Obviously, there is no political reason for India to move toward such a situation even at a future date, especially since its bilateral relations with the United States are likely to keep gaining strength on the basis of economic-trade relations between one of the two largest markets of the world on one side and the largest economy on the other.

In substance, therefore, India would hardly be giving up anything for access to what has come to be known as the trinity items, that is, access to dual-technology systems, nuclear power, and space programme for civilian purposes. But the bit-by-bit approach certainly adds to India's diplomatic leverages even if the overall process would take time. (In a similar way, non-proliferation linearity had strengthened India's diplomatic leverages by introducing the entry into force clause being contingent to India's accession.) In relation to nuclear power, the only difficulty that it poses is that the growth of nuclear power capacity in India would be slower. But in the process it would also be less sensitive to the international denial regimes. India can afford to wait. But greater access to nuclear power at an early date would help to speed up socio-economic growth. And the United States and other members of the G-8 have to decide whether they wish to be partners in this historic development or not.

Another approach would be to address issues at the ad hoc regimes without seeking changes in international treaties and/or national laws. This could be achieved by reexamining the NSG Guidelines and their applicability in country-specific cases. Manpreet Sethi, in her chapter in this book has made a strong case for why this should be done in the case of India. It is also significant that Strobe Talbot admits that even in the immediate aftermath of the 1998 nuclear tests and consequent sanctions on India, the support for sustaining those sanctions among the G-8 countries had eroded and "solid support came only from Japan and Canada" for the US hardline negotiating position. The French president had even gone to the extent of announcing a "strategic dialogue" with India by September 1998. Japan's grand strategy of getting India to renounce its nuclear weapons had lost support and momentum very soon although sanctions remained in force. At the Tokyo Forum set by the Japanese government, people like Professor Joseph Nye (who had been strongly urging India's accession to the NPT and other non-proliferation means as a non-nuclear weapon state) had clearly stated in the very first meeting of the Tokyo Forum (end July 1998) that it would be useless to press India to renounce nuclear weapons, and what needed to be given high priority was to help India to make its nuclear arsenal safer even if it required transfer of technology like that in the PAL (Permissive Action Links) systems. How far the attitudes of other nations have changed may be judged by the fact that Japan recently indicated that it would support India's entry into the UN Security Council as a permanent member.

One of the five "benchmarks" laid down by the United States in 1998 for post-test sanctions to be lifted was that India support the early conclusion of the FMCT (Fissile Material Cut-Off Treaty) lying dormant at the Conference on Disarmament in Geneva. This route also holds out the promise of the reconciliation that we are examining. It may be recalled that India and the United States had co-sponsored the resolution in December 1993 at the UN for an FMCT to ban further production of fissile material for weapons. The progress at Geneva has been stuck not because of India's objections, but because of other countries, including the United States. However, now that the United States has agreed to support the treaty, albeit without any verification clauses, the treaty may yet see the light of day. While many in India, in and outside the government, are opposed to the FMCT on the grounds that it risks

India's nuclear weapons capability for defence and, secondly, that it is only an extension of the larger non-proliferation agenda, the reality is that if the treaty is shaped finally on the lines of the original resolution and excludes existing stocks of fissile material for weapons purposes, this would perhaps be the first legal arrangement that treats India at par with the acknowledged nuclear weapon states by recognising its stocks of weapons. Properly handled, this could become the basis of reconciling non-proliferation with the needs of nuclear power for faster human development in India.

The head of the IAEA has also been talking about control of nuclear fuel under international management in order to further the interests of nuclear power and non-proliferation worldwide. On the face of it, there would be objections on the grounds of sovereignty, etc. But in reality, this offers a new approach to meet our needs without undermining our defence needs. In a way, such an option would only be in tune with the larger trends of globalisation.

This raises another issue. There is a view that the most defining issue for the 21st century would be the tussle between those who stand for globalisation and all it involves and those who are opposed to it. In reality, that struggle would be decided by the success and failure of globalisation rather than merely the issue of its polarised outcome. India is moving toward globalisation carefully and in a calibrated manner even if at times specific issues get drowned in domestic political rhetoric. The role of India with its one billion plus population would be an important factor in this struggle. If globalisation starts to fail in India, it is less likely to be the winner in the broader defining issue facing humanity. On the other hand, its success in India, like the success of India's non-violent struggle for independence, which expedited the decolonisation process half a century ago, and India's grand experiment of transforming its large population into a modern prosperous nation through democratic principles and practices, would be a major factor contributing to a better world in the 21st century. Globalisation embedded in a country of a billion people on the march toward greater prosperity has greater chances of success if the international community is willing to be a partner in this process.

Notes

1. General K.M. Arif, *Working with Zia: Pakistan's Power Politics 1977-1988*, (Karachi: Oxford University Press, 1995), p. 431. Also see US Senate Committee on Foreign Relations, International Security and Development Cooperation Act of 1984, 98th Congress, 2nd session, 1984 Senate Report 98-400, pp. 7, 19, 58-59, 114.
2. Dr. Samar Mubarakmand, the Pakistani scientist in charge of Pakistan's nuclear tests in May 1998, cited in *The Gulf Today,* May 19, 1999.
3. International Atomic Energy Agency, *Strengthening of the Activities of the Agency's Technical Cooperation Activities,* Resolution adopted at the General Conference, October 1999.
4. White House Press Release, "President Bush Calls on Congress to Pass Energy Bill." Remarks by the President on Energy, Central Aluminium Company, Columbus, Ohio, October 30, 2003.
5. Nuclear Energy Institute, Washington, http://www.nei.org/index.asp?
6. Andrew Taylor, "Asia Turns to Fight Power Shortages," *Financial Times,* January 6, 2004.
7. For example, see *China: The Proliferation Primer,* A Majority Report of the International Security, Proliferation, and Federal Services Subcommittee, United States Senate Committee on Government Affairs, January 1998, Washington DC.
8. What is often ignored is that New Delhi did seek nuclear security guarantees from the United States and others in 1967 to enable it to sign the NPT, but such guarantees were not forthcoming.
9. Former US Under Secretary of States Strobe Talbot who was engaged in 14 rounds of dialogue with Indian Minister for External Affairs Jaswant Singh after the May 1998 nuclear tests by India, reflects extensively on the limited impact of sanctions in his book *Engaging India: Diplomacy, Democracy and the Bomb* (New Delhi: Penguin-Viking, 2004).
10. Talbot, Ibid., p. 231.
11. See Jasjit Singh "Nuclear Doctrine for Defence" in Jasjit Singh and Manpreet Sethi, *Nuclear Deterrence and Diplomacy* (New Delhi: Knowledge World, 2004), pp. 219-246.

1

Nuclear Power and Non-Proliferation: Need for Convergence

Opening Address by Shri Kanwal Sibal

Thank you very much for inviting me to this seminar. It is always a great pleasure to be with colleagues, and more so with colleagues who know more about the subject that one is talking about, which means quite an intellectual exchange on these subjects.

The topic that has been chosen for this seminar is indeed very relevant, because this was one of the key issues in our discussions with the French initially, and also the United States, that is, how to get around the whole issue of international cooperation in India's nuclear power sector. But before I speak a little bit about that, I would like to make a few general comments.

Firstly, the nuclear Non-Proliferation Treaty (NPT) is supposed to create a convergence between non-proliferation and the plans of countries to develop nuclear energy cycles. The whole basis of the NPT is: do not develop nuclear weapon technology, and you will be given access to civilian nuclear power. But, in fact, rather than creating a convergence, it has planted the seed of very serious conflict. So, in that sense, the topic itself is rather interesting and intellectually teasing.

One cannot say that a convergence can be easily brought about between nuclear non-proliferation and the energy requirements of countries. If there is going to be any convergence, I think India

---

Shri Kanwal Sibal is former Foreign Secretary and India's Ambassador-designate to Russia.

would be a test case. If, in the case of India, the US and other members of the Nuclear Suppliers' Group (NSG) can find a practical way to deal with a difficult situation, then, in that sense, we would say that after 36 years, a kind of convergence that we have been looking for between the goals of the NPT on the military side and its goals on the civilian side has been achieved.

Why has this conflict occurred? I need not tell this knowledgeable audience that the nuclear weapon powers have not honoured their part of the bargain. They have used the provisions of the NPT to push forward, to promote more and more stringently their policies of preventing any possibility of countries, other than the five nuclear weapon powers, gaining access to nuclear military technology, rather than developing mechanisms, technological or otherwise, of making available under controlled conditions, access to nuclear civilian technology, whether through the International Atomic Energy Agency (IAEA) or otherwise, resulting in the kind of stalemate that we see on the ground. In that sense, the NPT has been effectively used in the political, strategic and security sense to create an unequal and discriminatory world order. The NSG that has been set up, which is at the heart of the system, has denied India access to civil nuclear technology and this continues to be a serious setback for us.

If you take the case of India, we have been told time and again that India should begin a dialogue with the NSG, that such a dialogue itself would be a confidence building measure that would lessen international opposition to offers made initially by France to open the doors for international cooperation in India's nuclear power sector. But we have not fallen into that trap because the NSG consists of so many countries. There are countries in the NSG that can take a purely ideological position on this issue. They have no economic interest in the development of the nuclear power sector in the sense that France would have, or the United States would have, or Germany would have. They can take a purely ideological position and raise the spectre of a collapse of the entire non-proliferation order if India were to be given access to civilian nuclear technology, without insisting on proper fullscope safeguards. So, we have been looking at these efforts to have an India-NSG dialogue essentially as a ploy to get us to adhere to the NSG regime but not to give us any nuclear status, not open the doors of peaceful nuclear cooperation to us, but to push us, prod us, to observe the NSG controls. This dialogue is, therefore, not proceeding forward.

We know the issue of fullscope safeguards. We are aware of the reasons for opposing it. From our point of view, it is an irrational and illogical position. Accepting fullscope safeguards would mean giving up our nuclear weapon programme. We are a nuclear weapon power. It would only be logical, rational and realistic on the part of the international community, which otherwise wishes to engage us in a strategic dialogue and build a long-term strategic relationship with us, which values the role that India is going to play in the future, which sees India as a future pole in the multipolar order, that they should accept *de facto* India's nuclear weapon status and modify their approach accordingly.

We are willing to accept facility-specific safeguards, which we already do in relation to those of our nuclear power plants which have been built with international help. Several of our nuclear power plants are already under IAEA safeguards. So, facility-specific safeguards is something that we have practised, which we have offered.

We have also said that all our future nuclear reactors built with international help would be put under safeguards. We have tried to persuade our partners to see that it is in their interest to accept India's offer. If there is concern that the power segment of India's nuclear sector needs some form of safeguards, especially as India has widely publicised its future programme of developing the nuclear power sector, if there is concern that fissile material produced could help build up our weapon stocks, then clearly our future nuclear reactors should be put under safeguards. To that extent, the concern of the international community about India's nuclear sector gets reduced.

We have also made some other proposals about our future nuclear power plants as a demonstration of our willingness to allay the concerns of the international community. We have shown a readiness to make some political gestures in order to encourage others to open the doors for international cooperation in India's civilian nuclear sector.

But the point is that nothing has taken off. The regrettable aspect is that despite some quite solid long-term proposals made by us within our constraints, which we have and which are very clear, there is no progress on this front. There is no question of India giving up its nuclear weapon status or capacity. I think we have gone as far as we could politically to create a basis for a serious effort on the part of the international community to see how to modify the NSG regime and find some practical way of cooperating with the Indian civilian nuclear sector. But it has not happened.

With the French, some efforts are being made. I was ambassador there, and know that very serious discussions have been held with the French. They are clearly interested in this subject at a very high level. I think one of the principal goals of the French is, and remains, cooperation in India's civil nuclear sector. However, they have been constrained by two things. One is the fact that they are themselves signatories to various agreements. They also have a very strong non-proliferation group, heavily influenced by their American counterparts. They are raising the same kind of concerns about the possibility of a very negative impact on the international nuclear structure if they go ahead and cooperate with India. Secondly, and equally importantly, they do not want to generate a controversy, a serious controversy, with the United States.

We have, therefore, adopted a kind of a via media approach, where we are going ahead and discussing with them the possibilities of cooperation in this sector, at both the technical and financial levels, and keeping ourselves in readiness as much as possible for the day when the doors are opened. The idea is that if we go ahead and keep everything in readiness, then, when the doors are opened, we could walk in and save a lot of time. The French are aware that the key lies with the United States of America and if at any time the door is opened, there would be very strong competition from them, and the French could be disadvantaged if they do not prepare the basis of future cooperation with us. There is some very good cooperation going on at the ground level between our atomic energy establishment and the French Commissariat of Atomic Energy. We have identified several areas of technical cooperation under the rubric of safety; whether under the rubric of safety we can get them to transfer technology to us is another matter.

So, at the moment we are stuck with the situation that the French are willing to wound and yet afraid to strike. They want to go ahead but also do not want to take on the Americans. So, they tell us that at the political level the atmosphere is favourable and that we should talk to the United States, and that from their side they would also be talking at the highest levels there.

This leads me to the subject of what we have been trying to do with the United States in this field. Our own approach to the United States is to come out and talk to them on this issue in a more forthright manner. I would like to take a little credit for having initiated this dialogue with the United States in a proactive manner, rather than let them dictate to us what they can and cannot do in this area. We have submitted our thoughts in very concise terms of what we expect from the US, if they wish to build a long-term strategic relationship with us. Our argument is that you cannot build a long-term strategic relationship unless you get the strategic issues out of the way. These are real strategic issues which go to the heart of India's nuclear status, its standing in the international community, and its relationship with all the restrictive regimes in place.

The technology denial regimes that have been set up, which

heavily colour the US' approach to South Asia, which, in turn, is heavily influenced by the nuclear equations in South Asia, are very germane to India's aspiration to become a permanent member of the UN Security Council. Once we are able, in some way, to overcome the real problem posed by the denial regimes, then, in a strategic sense, our relationship with the United States will take off on a trajectory which is very different from what it is today. It is absurd to say that India and the United States can be strategic partners if, in furtherance of its strategic goals, the United States applies sanctions to India, and in effect, treats India as some kind of "a more respectable rogue state." So, there is a real problem here.

I must say that our dialogue with the United States has begun well. There seems to be genuine commitment at the levels of the White House to see some practical way out without affecting the larger global perspective that the United States has about the basis of civilian nuclear cooperation with other countries. If we can go beyond the safety-oriented dialogue that has been embarked upon in the past with the United States, this could open the door progressively to international cooperation in India's civilian sector. I think one should not underestimate the importance of the United States publicly, saying at the level of the president and the secretary of state that India and the United States are exploring the possibility of cooperating more in India's civilian nuclear energy programme, space programme and the like. This is a big change in attitude on the part of the United States.

We have made some progress. We had a sudden visit by US Deputy National Security Adviser Hadley to India when, after a series of confabulations at a very high level within the US government, he proposed a "glide path" for implementation which would require reciprocal actions by both sides in these sensitive sectors, entailing more US cooperation in India's civilian nuclear and space programmes. Naturally, we had a few questions to ask. The dialogue has been pursued, leading ultimately to the joint statement by President Bush and Prime Minister Vajpayee in January this year, reflecting the core objectives of this bilateral exercise. On the contents of that "glide path," there are three or four observations that I would like to make.

The first is that any feeling that the doors to international cooperation in India's civil nuclear sector are going to be opened soon by the US is not well founded. But what is going on would certainly be a significant step forward in terms of US involvement in the nuclear establishment of India. It is clear that whatever the US is debarred from doing by law, they would not do. Whatever they are not doing because of policy, that also would not be entirely reviewed. But some progress would be made of the kind that will avoid any problems with the US Congress, that they would be able to defend before the NSG or anybody else, should any questions be raised.

So, it is a less than fully satisfactory situation from our point of view but it is a step forward on a difficult subject. Realistically, this issue cannot be resolved shortly. Therefore, there is a case to move forward incrementally and do whatever can be done to break the rigidity of the Western position and use that as a platform for building more on that later on.

On the civilian space sector, I must say that the possibilities are a little more substantial. The issues involved there are less complicated. There is no non-proliferation treaty in the space sector, as it is on the nuclear side.

We have asked whether it has now become a "glide path." The answer is "yes" and "no". Yes, because the level of attention which is being devoted to this dossier has gone down. The White House does not want to expend too much time on this now. We have been pressing that on the US side, the White House should further this process and it should be done at the level of Deputy National Security Adviser Hadley. The US has taken the decision that it will be Christina Rocca who would be the point person, which is clearly unsatisfactory for more than one reason. Most importantly, the matter gets into the lap of the State Department, and in the State Department it gets into the lap of the non-proliferation diehards. A couple of issues remain unsolved.

One is end use verification, which, when I was there, was on the verge of being resolved satisfactory. But, now, they say that the last end use verification was unsatisfactory, after having told us initially that it was one of the most successful that they had ever done. They want more unfettered access but we want the process to be guided by arrangements acceptable to us. There is also the issue of non-proliferation. Our record is clean in this regard and the US has to find a way to deal with this issue with us on terms different from those countries which have a dubious record on non-proliferation. We now have a change in government. This is a complicated subject which raises very vital political issues; a change in government and the new incumbents taking up the thread and taking some time to understand the pros and cons and the subtleties of the issues, is going to lead to some delay in pursuing the process.

I want to make some brief comments on one or two issues. One is that the Americans bracket India and Pakistan as far as proliferation questions are concerned. On several things that we are discussing with them, the United States has not taken decisions vis-à-vis India because of the effect on Pakistan. The US, of course, distrusts Pakistan, a distrust reinforced by all the news that has surfaced, including the confessions made by the Pakistani leadership. There is perhaps greater disinclination in the US to give the same degree of acceptance to Pakistan as to India in the nuclear area. On the other hand, they will not separate India and Pakistan. So, this is the Gordian knot, which has to be cut.

I would have thought that the Pakistani confessions, which are very serious ones in terms of US concerns about weapons of mass destruction (WMD) falling into the hands of non-state actors and terrorists or whatever, could have been exploited by us to push the United States into separating its policy toward India and Pakistan. The basis of the Pakistani position is that Pakistan's nuclear policy is a reaction to what India does. However, when they supply nuclear weapon technology and designs to Iran, Libya or others, the India factor is not there at all. And these Pakistani actions are directly against the US interests. There are Islamic connections in this. This is a wholly different ball game, which has nothing to do with the India and Pakistan equation. The real problem to the Western security comes from these actions.

Secondly, the United States wants us increasingly to become a part of the global non-proliferation architecture that they have set up. On our side, there is inclination to demonstrate our good faith and cooperate as much as possible with the international community in the area of non-proliferation, so that we are not looked down upon as bad boys. After we have acquired nuclear weapon status, nuclear weapon capability, we want to bury the past image of India as a spoiler as far as the non-proliferation scenario is concerned. So, we have wanted to be positive in our approach.

Now as regards the Proliferation Security Initiative, we may find it possible to support it provided our nuclear weapon status is recognised. It is much easier for us to be part of—even if it is inconsistent with our past position—it is much easier for us to cooperate more and more on non-proliferation in a practical, pragmatic manner and not focus on the inherently discriminatory nature of the arrangements, which is a fact, if our nuclear status is clearer.

One way this can be done, to my mind, without the United States fearing that the international structure of non-proliferation might be destroyed, is to open the door to international cooperation in India's nuclear power sector, on the basis of on-going discussions, taking into account the environmental concerns, which have been spelt out earlier. This is the right moment to delink India and Pakistan. So, without any formal acceptance of India's nuclear power status, etc, this gesture of cooperation in India's nuclear power sector would make it far easier for us to cooperate with the US and other countries in further reinforcing the non-proliferation architecture. But we have shied away from exploiting Pakistan's very damaging confessions to our advantage.

What do we bring to the Americans in this exercise? To my mind, we bring a very vital thing to the Americans, in that India, which has been intellectually the most powerful, the most coherent opponent of the discriminatory non-proliferation order, would give its imprimatur to it. So, in a sense, we would help make the nuclear non-proliferation architecture more respectable, in both the moral and political sense. So there is a bargain that can be made.

Thank you!

2

Nuclear Disorder

Matin Zuberi

The global nuclear order has rested on two mutually supportive arrangements—the elaborate structure of nuclear deterrence and the non-proliferation regime. A rough equality of military power was measured in terms of assured destruction. And uneven distribution of military nuclear capabilities assured rank ordering of nuclear weapon powers. This balance of terror created some semblance of order based primarily on the unprecedented common interest of all states in avoiding a nuclear holocaust. Paradoxically, nuclear restraint was ultimately grounded in the possibility of a lack of restraint. Moreover, rapid sequences of technological innovation and obsolescence constantly undermined the balance of terror. Arms control was designed to make the world safe for nuclear deterrence by providing a measure of predictability in deterrent relationships.

To be sure, the nuclear shadow fell over the entire globe. The structure of nuclear deterrence, however, operated in the context of the rival military blocs and the non-proliferation regime covered the non-nuclear weapon states signatory to the nuclear Non-Proliferation Treaty (NPT). Member states of the rival blocs that had renounced the nuclear weapon option provided a link between the two arrangements. With this exception, nuclear deterrence was excluded from the regions where the non-proliferation regime operated. Nuclear weapon powers eschewed the use of nuclear weapons through the so-called Negative Security Assurances.

Dr. Matin Zuberi is Professor Emeritus, SIS, Jawaharlal Nehru University, New Delhi.

As for nuclear deterrence, it was assumed that decision-makers in the international system would continue to be guided by the rational calculus of their national interests. Nuclear deterrence, it is now feared, may not provide the comfort it did during the Cold War. The Soviet threat, it is now conceded, came from a well-organised, rational group of countries that were part of Western civilisation and culture. They "loved their children, too, and they could, therefore, be deterred." The Cold War confrontation, Eliot Cohen has observed, was between a "stable and contented democracy" and "a highly rational, cautious dictatorship that found nothing shameful about retreating in the face of superior force." It was, in many ways, "an ideal opposition." Reckless "rogue" regimes led by tyrants may not buy into the old deterrence theory. There is talk of deterrence by the strong of the crazy. National missile defence is, therefore, needed to cope with this new threat. This assessment, however, is based on debatable assumptions. As Lawrence Freedman has pointed out, it is assumed that responsible leaders of those regimes are crazy—"Hitler-in-his-bunker sort of scenario."

There has been an exponential growth in the accuracy and lethality of precision-guided munitions. Only six years ago, the quintessential nuclear hawk, Paul Nitze, advocated conversion of the American strategic deterrent from nuclear to conventional weapons. Instead, nuclear weapons with low yields are being developed for battlefield use, especially in response to chemical or biological attacks by "rogue" states. A British jurist asserted during hearings on the legality of nuclear weapons at the International Court of Justice that nuclear weapons could be used in a variety of circumstances "with very different results in terms of civilian casualties." Josef Rotblat has perceptively observed that the new US Nuclear Posture Review discards "the previous doctrine of nuclear weapons being viewed as weapons of last resort, and spells out a strategy which incorporates nuclear capability into conventional war planning." It specifically enumerates Iran, Iraq, Libya, North Korea and Syria as potential targets of US nuclear weapons in certain contingencies.

The nuclear non-proliferation regime is an interlocking network of international treaties, domestic legislation, bilateral, regional and multilateral verification systems called "nuclear safeguards," positive and negative security assurances, economic sanctions, technology controls, and nuclear weapon-free zones. The central pillar of this regime is the NPT with its nodal agency being the International Atomic Energy Agency (IAEA). It was initially an imposed order with inherent inequalities. "This is," assured Secretary of State John Foster Dulles, "essentially a made-in-America project."

The original objective of NPT safeguards was "the timely detection of diversion of significant quantities of nuclear material from peaceful nuclear facilities to the manufacture of nuclear weapons or other nuclear explosive devices or for purposes unknown, and deterrence of such diversion by the risk of early detection." The terms "manufacture," "nuclear weapons," or "other nuclear explosives" were not defined. "Significant quantities of nuclear material," however, were defined as 8 kg of plutonium and 25 kg of enriched uranium. In order to protect the commercial interests of the industrialised non-nuclear weapon countries, the human element of inspection is reduced to the barest minimum. Safeguards applied to the nuclear material and the facilities through which it passed were listed in a subsidiary agreement between the IAEA and the state concerned. Provision was also made for "material unaccounted for." As Japanese nuclear expert Ryukichi Imai once put it: "The amount of material unaccounted for could total 10 to 50 bombs every six months."

The NPT had not prohibited the development of enrichment and reprocessing facilities so long as they were under safeguards. Reprocessing was generally considered a necessary component of an efficient fuel cycle, an essential step in nuclear waste disposal and a logical move toward the projected development of a "plutonium economy" through the development of breeder reactors. Noble Laureate Glenn T. Seaborg, a former chairman of the US Atomic Energy Commission, was a great promoter of the plutonium economy. Unilaterally reversing the direction set by the United States for global nuclear technological development in decades of American leadership, President Ford declared on October 28, 1976: *"I have decided* that the United States should no longer regard reprocessing of used nuclear fuel to produce plutonium as a necessary and inevitable step in the nuclear fuel cycle." He also asked all concerned governments to affirm that they would regard *"nuclear wrongdoing* as an intolerable violation of acceptable norms of acceptable behaviour, which would set in motion strong and immediate countermeasures." The Carter Administration embarked on a wholesale change in the future direction of civilian nuclear technology. According to the new policy, plutonium reprocessing and breeder reactors were no longer inevitable parts of the nuclear fuel cycle. The US Nuclear Non-Proliferation Act of 1978 provided for renegotiation of all nuclear contracts with foreign countries and mandated fullscope safeguards as a condition for nuclear transactions. It also unilaterally extended US jurisdiction to cover any nuclear fuel, regardless of origin, utilised in a reactor or facility, partially or fully supplied by the United States. If, for example, Namibian uranium were used in an American-supplied Japanese reactor, US jurisdiction would extend over it as if the United States had supplied it. This nuclear revisionism entailing unilateral changes in multilateral accords did not go down well with the West Europeans and the Japanese. The proposal to renegotiate existing cooperative agreements while commitments under these agreements were not being fulfilled was viewed as contrary to the assurances of reliability of supply and further contributed to the erosion of confidence. The Japanese resented the American posture of a "God-granted guardian" of nuclear technology and the tendency to ignore history.

The NPT only made a distinction between nuclear weapon powers and non-nuclear weapon countries. Another layer of discrimination was later added—non-nuclear weapon countries that were free to develop enrichment, reprocessing, and breeder technologies and others that were allowed only a fragmented nuclear fuel cycle. This unilateral attempt to change the rules of the game could not be tolerated and there was uproar in Western Europe and Japan. The military allies/commercial competitors of the United States simply refused to accept this new definition of non-proliferation. They went ahead with reprocessing where they had an advantage over the United States. They also broke the American monopoly over the supply of enriched uranium. Among the non-nuclear weapon states signatory to the NPT, Germany and Japan now have large inventories of separated plutonium under IAEA safeguards.

By the late 1970s, the definition of proliferation changed from acquiring nuclear weapons or other explosive devices to developing a "nuclear explosive capability." Consequently, the objective of safeguards changed from early detection of diversion of significant quantities of nuclear materials from peaceful to military pursuits to "prevention of development of nuclear explosive capability." This change in the objective of safeguards was contrary to their original purpose. Myron Kratzer, an American architect of the NPT safeguards system, had categorically stated that the safeguards system was "never intended to be a system for the prevention of diversion." He added that "if an IAEA inspector saw someone walking out of a plant with nuclear material, he would not have the slightest authority to stop him." The occurrence could only be reported to the IAEA that would, in turn, report to the UN Security Council for action.

A resurgence of restrictive approaches following the Gulf War led to further tightening of the non-proliferation regime. Until the early 1990s, safeguards covered only the nuclear facilities and materials listed in the subsidiary agreement with the IAEA. They were not designed to detect clandestine nuclear facilities and material. According to Herbert Scoville, the IAEA was not "an international espionage organisation" with the right "to roam over a country to locate clandestine nuclear plants." Revelations about the Iraqi nuclear weapons programme led to criticism of the IAEA safeguards. What Iraq had done, however, was to develop a covert nuclear fuel cycle that did not intersect with its declared facilities that were regularly inspected. The Director of the IAEA Hans Blix conceded in an article published by the United Nations in 1993 that "Iraq did not divert any material for its weapons programme." The industrialised countries that had in the past opposed an intrusive verification system, now favoured it. Ironically, these were the countries that had profited from nuclear exports to Iraq. They wanted verification efforts shifted away from countries with large civilian fuel cycles to what they called "suspect" countries. The IAEA Board of Governors decided in 1992 to assert the right of "special inspections" of any nuclear facility in a country under IAEA safeguards.

The objective of safeguards was again changed in 1992 to "prevention of the transfer of capabilities for use in a non-nuclear-weapon state in a nuclear explosive activity or an unsafeguarded nuclear fuel cycle activity." In a major departure from the original NPT safeguards, the IAEA can now use the National Technical Means of member states to locate undeclared nuclear material and facilities in an inspected state. New sensitive techniques for sampling rivers and the atmosphere to trace isotopes indicating clandestine operations are to be used by IAEA inspectors. "Country profiles" of what are called "sensitive" countries are being prepared. These successive changes in the definition of proliferation and the further tightening of the verification procedures have been broadly accepted by the inspected states, and the non-proliferation regime is, thus, no longer an imposed one. The Model Protocol Additional Safeguards Agreement of 1997 has further tightened the IAEA safeguards. Iran's adherence to it is presently being negotiated by the IAEA.

The coercive and comprehensive disarmament of Iraq under the mandate of the UN Security Council is unique in the history of disarmament. Successive resolutions of the Security Council indicted the oppressive regime of Saddam Hussein for lack of cooperation in this endeavour. Despite Anglo-American dissatisfaction with the pace of verified destruction of Iraqi weapons, however, it has been the most comprehensive, though incomplete, disarmament of any country under the auspices of the United Nations. The Iraqi nuclear weapons programme was dismantled and all fissile material taken out of the country. There has been no evidence so far of its attempted revival. The inspectors did not achieve a similar success with regard to all Iraqi chemical and biological weapons and equipment. The Iraqi case has raised a number of troubling questions about the effectiveness of the verification procedures; even more troubling was the dubious intelligence supplied to the Security Council by the United States and Britain. North Korea has posed the most serious challenge to the entire non-proliferation regime by withdrawing from the NPT and expelling the IAEA inspectors.

The regime was initially based on the premise of technical hurdles in the production of fissile material. Instead of the anticipated scarcity, however, there is now a surfeit of it. It is estimated that the "excess" plutonium from dismantled warheads and plutonium separated from spent reactor fuel is sufficient for about 9,000 and 25,000 nuclear weapons respectively. The Royal Society of Britain warned in 1998 that even in a country as stable as Britain, the possibility that the stocks of civil plutonium might be seized for illicit weapons production was of extreme concern. Francesco Calogero has highlighted the dangers of terrorists producing a working bomb with highly enriched uranium. It is a sad commentary on the non-proliferation regime that only about 30 per cent of this plutonium and less than one per cent of highly enriched uranium are safeguarded by the IAEA.

The two arrangements that sustained the nuclear order are no longer exclusive in their operation. The United States as the chief architect of this nuclear order has succeeded in making substantial changes in the non-proliferation regime. Arms control that provided a link between nuclear deterrence and the non-proliferation regime is now viewed as a relic of the Cold War. With possibilities of a nuclear response to a chemical or biological attack from countries that were previously part of the non-proliferation regime, there is a danger of nuclear disorder. An international consensus exists on the campaign against terrorism. There is, however, considerable unease about combining it with preventive or preemptive counter-proliferation. The nuclear order has survived so far because of the strengthening of the taboo against the military use of nuclear weapons during each successive decade of the nuclear era. Any such use, accidental or deliberate, would destroy whatever remains of that order.

---

* The paper was also presented at the 53rd Pugwash Conference: *Advancing Human Security: The Role of Technology and Politics,* Halifax, Nova Scotia, Canada, July 17-21, 2003. It was published under the title "Uncertain Future: NPT and the Global Nuclear Order," in *RUSI Journal,* vol. 148, no. 6, December 2003, pp. 42-45.

3

Nuclear Flux? The Future of Nuclear Weapons and Proliferation

Rajesh Rajagopalan

The current international nuclear order is thought to be changing dramatically. There are several sources of such dramatic changes. At one end of the spectrum, the nuclear non-proliferation regime, we are led to believe, is under tremendous strain, with several members of the nuclear Non-Proliferation Treaty (NPT) on the verge of breaking out of the regime. In the meantime, new threats have arisen—that of terrorists, using stolen or otherwise illegally acquired nuclear material or even weapons, who seem poised to use them to create unimaginable havoc. At the other end of the spectrum, even the limited progress achieved in nuclear arms control after the Cold War ended appears under challenge as the existing nuclear powers experiment with new types of small nuclear weapons that could erase the distinction between nuclear and conventional arms.

If all of the above were indeed to happen, we would truly be in a nuclear era, one marked by great turbulence compared to the relatively stable order that characterised the first half-century of the nuclear order. But though the international nuclear order is under some challenge, I would argue that the nuclear order will change in about the same manner that it has changed until now, which is to say, very slowly. Nevertheless, this is also a 'large-picture' view: there are likely to be interesting modifications at the

Dr. Rajesh Rajagopalan is Associate Professor in International Politics, Jawaharlal Nehru University, New Delhi.

edges of the nuclear order. While not fundamentally changing the international nuclear order, it does promise to make international nuclear politics more interesting and open opportunities for Indian policy.

The Future of the Nuclear Order

One way to look at the future of the nuclear order is to look at the possibility of extreme developments and see if such extremes are possible. The two possible extremes in this case are nuclear disarmament and its opposite, the collapse of the nuclear non-proliferation order and the large-scale spread of nuclear weapons to countries that do not have them.

The primary reason that nuclear disarmament will not happen in the foreseeable future is that disarmament is unlikely when only a few powerful countries have access to such technologies. This might appear paradoxical and counter-intuitive, and it goes against conventional wisdom. But the histories of arms control measures do provide some support to this thesis. Chemical and biological weapons have been a significant threat for over a century, but the push to finally abolish these weapons took place only after the technology to produce these weapons had spread to a significant number of countries, especially in the developing world. In fact, both chemical and biological weapons programmes are far harder to detect than nuclear weapons, thus, making verification procedures much more cumbersome and intrusive than for nuclear weapons. Nevertheless (despite the political difficulties facing the Biological Weapons Convention), both treaties were concluded in the 1990s. Thus, the argument frequently trotted by some countries about verification and 'breakouts' being too great a threat to conclude a nuclear disarmament treaty are not valid.

But such a spread is unlikely to happen with nuclear weapons. This is not so much because nuclear weapons are high-technology; they are not. The only real mystery about nuclear weapons was whether they would work, and there has been little doubt about that for the last half-century. The general principles of building nuclear weapons are well known; even the engineering skill required to build one is today not difficult to manage. The real obstacle remains the material needed, both fissilc material and other kinds of material. These materials are rare and tightly controlled, though there have been suspicions about leakages.

The Future of the NPT Regime

It has become fashionable, yet again, to predict the collapse of the NPT regime. The last time such a debate happened was in the aftermath of the Indian and Pakistani nuclear tests in the summer of 1998. Now, North Korea's apparent breakout of the NPT Treaty, and Iran's challenge to the NPT regime are leading to yet another debate about the future of the regime.

The regime is not about to collapse. It will survive even if both North Korea and Iran manage successful breakouts from the NPT. It will survive because the success and failure of international regimes depend almost exclusively on the patronage of the dominant powers in the international system, not on the acquiescence of the weakest of its members. In fact, as in the past, any successful breakout by North Korea and Iran will only lead to a more stringent regime, more intrusive inspections to prevent future surprises and greater penalties for those attempting to violate the regime.

There are, of course, conditions under which the international system might accept the decline and demise of an international regime. The balance of power might change in the international system, and a new power, with different interests, could emerge, leading to the collapse of the regime. The European colonial system collapsed partly because the new hegemons in the post-1945 period were unwilling to support it. Could a new hegemon rise which will junk the NPT system? Don't bet on it. The NPT system legitimises and preserves a serious imbalance of power in the international system between those who have nuclear weapons and those who don't. A new hegemon will most likely (though not necessarily) see its benefits, just as the old hegemon did. Remember the violent Chinese opposition to the NPT regime as it was negotiated, and their stellar defence of it today, as China becomes increasingly part of the hegemonic coterie in the international system? Of course, there is yet another problem with this scenario: there is little likelihood of a new hegemon in the foreseeable future.

Alternatively, the international system could evolve into the much hoped-for 'multipolar' system, with several powers of roughly equal power dominating it. Such a system could eventually develop (it would be a while though), and the competition between the dominant powers in such a system could provide sufficient space for the weak to slowly whittle away at the edges of the system. India and Pakistan did so in the 1970s and 1980s, as both the Soviet Union and the US, adamantly anti-proliferationist otherwise, found that other bipolar strategic interests trumped their anti-proliferationist tendencies. Though this could happen, the prospect of a new global multipolar order will take decades to develop.

If the NPT regime is to collapse, the most likely scenario is that the existing hegemon will change its view of its national interest. Washington, very conceivably, could decide that the NPT regime is no longer in its interest. This could happen not because the Bush Administration suddenly decides that "more may be better," but because they will see the NPT as a typically useless multilateral arms control process that cannot prevent proliferation. If Washington were to decide that they would rather trust the US military to do the job that the International Atomic Energy Agency (IAEA) cannot, then the NPT regime would be dead. Iran and North Korea may still be responsible for this collapse, but not in the way they are being characterised in the current debate about the NPT's future.

This last possibility has appeared more likely in the recent past. On February 11, 2004, President George Bush called for a major change to the NPT to close what he said was a "loophole" in the NPT. The "loophole" is one of the two central bargains in the NPT: that non-nuclear weapon states (NNWS) that voluntarily gave up their right to build nuclear weapons will be allowed to benefit from the peaceful atom, access to civilian nuclear technology. The other bargain was that countries that do not have nuclear weapons will not acquire nuclear weapons in exchange for countries that have nuclear weapons eventually giving them up.

In addition, President Bush argued for other measures to strengthen the NPT regime: an expansion of the Proliferation Security Initiative (PSI), which seeks international interdiction of underground nuclear trafficking; strengthening of domestic laws to criminalise proliferation; and curtailing of civilian nuclear transfers to only those countries that have signed the Additional Protocol to the NPT, which allows for far more intrusive inspections by the IAEA than permitted by the original NPT. He also proposed an expansion of the Nunn-Lugar programme, which pays for retraining of former Soviet nuclear scientists so that they are not tempted by the nuclear black market, to cover also other ex-states of concern, such as Iraq and Libya, and countries such as Iran, which are under investigation for proliferation violations.

The next day, Mohamed El Baradei, director-general of the IAEA, in an essay in the *New York Times,* argued that the NPT regime needs to be toughened. He called for greater control over fissile material, and more power to the IAEA through the Additional Protocol to conduct instrusive inspections, but many of his other recommendations went beyond what President Bush had called for. This included progress in the second bargain in the NPT between the nuclear powers and the NNWS about eventual nuclear disarmament, and forward movement on the Comprehensive Test Ban Treaty (CTBT) and Fissile Missile Control Talks (FMCT), both of which are frozen for different reasons. Most critically, and controversially, he called for elimination of the right to withdrawal from the NPT, a fundamental right under most international treaties.

These are not new thoughts. There have been continuing concerns in Washington and other capitals about loopholes in the non-proliferation regime. Many of the subsidiary agreements that together make up the non-proliferation 'regime,' such as the Nuclear Suppliers Group (NSG), Missile Technology Control Regime (MTCR), etc., came up as a consequence of what the nuclear powers felt were failures of the non-proliferation regime. Over the last year, partly as a consequence of the revelations by North Korea, Libya and Iran, there has been increased talk of further tightening of the regime. Despite the fact that none of these powers acquired nuclear weapons technology by diverting civilian nuclear technology, but rather by deliberate proliferation by a nuclear weapon state, the focus has been on tightening of controls on civilian nuclear technology.

Some of these ideas are not new. It is clear, in retrospect, that these ideas were being discussed seriously among US policy analysts. For example, Ashton Carter, a Harvard-based scholar with extensive links with both the Clinton and the Bush Administrations, wrote in a joint essay in December in the *New York Times* that even those countries that are members of the NPT should not be permitted to have a nuclear fuel cycle, because even a civilian capacity to produce nuclear fuel can translate into a military programme to build nuclear weapons. Controlling indigenous nuclear fuel production technology, thus, has antecedents.

The problem is that this does not address the real issue: all the countries that have acquired nuclear weapons, or have come close to it, were able to do so only because of covert external assistance, not because they managed to successfully subvert civilian programmes. Without this external support, they would not have reached where they are. These proposals do not address this particular problem.

Pakistan's Proliferation and its Implications

Much of the recent concern about the NPT regime and attempts at modifying the NPT regime can be traced to the recent revelations about what has come to be known as Pakistan's nuclear super-bazaar. Pakistan has, as New Delhi had suspected for quite a while, been using its skill in poking holes through the nuclear technology trade barriers to buy itself money and equipment that it needed from other potential proliferators such as North Korea, Iran and Libya. But despite being caught red-handed, Pakistan's proliferation activities might not cease. Other than a promise to curtail future proliferation activities, Pakistan will offer nothing to the international community, and the international community (read Washington) will settle for this because of Pakistan's perceived importance to Washington in fighting the war on terror. There are several conditions under which we could see a full-scale resumption of Pakistan's proliferation activities. If Pakistan's politics should move further rightward, and the religious fundamentalist parties should become more powerful in Islamabad, they might be tempted to restart such transfers, both for ideological reasons as well as to assert Pakistan's independence from Washington. More likely, if Pakistan needs specific technologies for its strategic programme, it might be tempted to pay for such programmes with its nuclear technology, as it has done in the past when it traded its nuclear technology for North Korean missiles. More improbably, if Pakistan faces a serious financial crunch, nuclear proliferation might provide a way to earn hard currency. There is some indication that financial incentives motivated at least some of Pakistan's proliferation activities in the past. Lastly, individual Pakistani scientists or small coteries may attempt to proliferate for reasons of money as well as ideology, or more likely both. Though Pakistan has attempted to defend itself from charges of proliferation by asserting these were not state directed activities but individual transgressions, this has been met with much well deserved scepticism. Nevertheless, it is possible that in future such transgressions could take place. They will be more difficult to detect and stop.

Consequences of Pakistan's Proliferation

One definite consequence of Pakistan's activities will be a tightening of US and general international technology control regulations. President George Bush, in his speech on February 11, has already announced that he would seek tighter controls on nuclear and other sensitive high-technology exports. This will hamper the recent progress made by India and the US on technology transfers on areas of mutual interests such as civilian nuclear and space technology. American and Western non-proliferation activities are bound to demand greater vigilance on proliferation-related activities and greater controls and restrictions on technology flows. In addition, the US will expect India, and other countries, to further tighten domestic regulations on technology export controls. This is already an issue in US-India bilateral discussions; its salience can now be expected to increase.

Modifying the NPT Regime

New Delhi should encourage the NPT system to take a second look at admitting acknowledged nuclear powers such as India, Pakistan and Israel, into the NPT system as nuclear weapon states (NWS). Such inclusion will require all three new nuclear powers to shoulder the responsibilities of the non-proliferation regime, and it would help get over the current anomaly of three of the world's nuclear powers, living in very dangerous, and possibly unstable neighbourhoods, being outside the responsibilities and supervision of the regime. The non-proliferation fundamentalists in Washington who want India, Pakistan and Israel to join the NPT as non-nuclear states will surely oppose such a move, which they see as rewarding the proliferators. But if Pakistan had been under the NPT umbrella after 1998, even as an NWS, its proliferation would have violated its legal international obligations rather than just normative restraints.

One technical objection to adding to the count of NWS in the NPT is that the treaty defines NWS as those that had nuclear weapons before 1967. But this can be easily resolved with an additional protocol to the NPT. As of now, the primary obstacle to the inclusion of the *de facto* nuclear powers is political, not legal.

Conclusion

In essence, then, there is unlikely to be much movement at the extremes of the nuclear order. There is neither likely to be any dramatic shift towards nuclear disarmament, nor is there likely to be any rapid increase in the number of nuclear weapon states in the world. The nuclear order is unlikely to look very different two decades from now, just as it is today not very different from two decades back. It is easy to predict that the P-5 will stay as nuclear powers: the United States, Russia, China, Britain and France. The three *de facto* nuclear powers, India, Pakistan and Israel, the so-called D-3, are also likely to remain as they are. They are unlikely to give up their nuclear weapons, so there is little prospect that the numbers would shrink. But there is a likelihood that one or more states might join the *de facto* category, in which case we could be looking at D-4, D-5, or even D-6. The final category, the wanna-be states such as North Korea, Iran, and possibly Japan, could expand. Some states, such as Japan and Germany, clearly have the potential to build their own nuclear arsenals. A generation later, as the salience of the misdeeds of the World War II generation in these countries wanes, it is possible that they could become far less reluctant to contemplate the acquisition of nuclear weapons.

But the pace of such changes will be slow. On an average, only one country has gone nuclear in the last seven or so decades. There is little to indicate that there is anything that can speed up this process. There is unlikely to be much change in the other direction either. Though there has been some dramatic reduction in the bloated Cold War nuclear arsenals, this change is far less dramatic than arms control agreements would lead us to believe. For example, though the US and Russia have agreed to bring their nuclear arsenals down to a couple of thousand nuclear warheads, both sides will maintain large numbers of weapons in various states of dismantlement, ready to be 'reconstituted' at very short notice should the situation so demand. For example, the latest nuclear arms control agreement between the US and Russia, which will bring the warheads on both sides to about 2,200, counts only "operationally deployed" weapons in this 2,200. This does not include the two Trident missile submarines (on the US side) which are expected to be in overhaul at any given time, which could carry as many as 240 warheads. The US Nuclear Posture Review calls for a "responsive force" which could be quickly deployed and which could include as many as 10,000 warheads. And, of course, all the nuclear powers are continuing to conduct weapons-related research.

Thus, we can rule out dramatic changes in the nuclear order. Much of the worry about a collapsing international nuclear order leading to nuclear anarchy is, thus, misplaced. The nuclear order can be expected to be as stable in the coming decades as it has been in the previous ones.

4

NSG Guidelines: Need for a Country-Specific Approach

Manpreet Sethi

Introduction

The primary objective of the Nuclear Suppliers Group (NSG) is to ensure that the suppliers uniformly apply a comprehensive set of guidelines so that nuclear cooperation does not result in proliferation. Like other countries that are party to the NSG, India too, even though outside the group, is genuinely concerned about proliferation of nuclear weapons. Situated as it is in a proliferation prone neighbourhood, this reality is more than apparent to New Delhi and it fully comprehends the dangers of unbridled nuclear proliferation.

At the same time, though, India maintains that for countries that have or envision a huge demand for electricity in the coming years, and that wish to exploit the nuclear option for their energy security, access to peaceful use of nuclear energy is necessary for economic and social development. This is particularly important now as heightened sensitivity to environmental concerns emphasises the need for compatibility between the methods of electricity generation and ecological sustainability. The international community is becoming increasingly aware of greenhouse gas (GHG) emissions from thermal power plants and their impact on the global climate. Nuclear reactors, on the other hand, are virtually

---

Dr. Manpreet Sethi is Senior Fellow, Centre for Strategic and International Studies, New Delhi.

GHG emissions-free. Therefore, using them to generate electricity, it is believed, can substantially help to arrest the dangers of global warming and radical climate change.[1]

Traditionally, export controls as enforced through the NSG, have sought to check nuclear proliferation by allowing or denying access to nuclear technology based on the perceived intent of the countries. This has been premised on their willingness to accept International Atomic Energy Agency (IAEA) safeguards and allow inspections and verification of all their nuclear facilities. The controls have been applied on the basis of certain guidelines, though the efficacy of these has always been questionable.[2] Treading a fine line between preventing acquisition of nuclear and dual-use technology, materials and knowhow for use in development of nuclear weapons, and allowing access for peaceful nuclear use has not been easy.

Enough evidence now points out that the NSG has not always been able to check nuclear proliferation. Rather, in many cases, its members have aided, abetted or turned a blind eye to certain nuclear exports to certain countries when it suited their interest.[3] On the other hand, NSG guidelines have hampered the development of a peaceful power programme in many countries. India is one such that has been affected by them. Despite having a responsible nuclear export policy, India is today a victim of the NSG guidelines. Access to nuclear reactors, technology, and materials is denied to it because New Delhi has refused to accept fullscope safeguards (FSS) on its nuclear programme. But India, having largely an indigenously developed peaceful power programme, has also considered it unnecessary to accept these. This stalemate, however, has imposed cost and time demands on India's peaceful nuclear advancements. Of course, the controls have neither been able to stop the weapons programme, nor have they been able to restrain the power programme. They have only managed to slow it down a bit.

This handicap is being increasingly felt in the present times as economic growth picks up, and future energy demand is expected to rise phenomenally. Nuclear energy, therefore, will have to be considered an important component in India's energy mix. However, for the requisite growth of nuclear energy in India, and to meet the Department of Atomic Energy's (DAE's) current planned target of 20,000 MWe by 2020, it would be important that the country be assured of:

(a) security of supply of nuclear materials and components;
(b) access to more efficient and newer reactor technologies;
(c) simpler and easier arrangements on importing nuclear reactors, materials and components.

Obviously, the major obstacle in the path of the above requirements comprises the NSG guidelines. Owing to India's position on FSS, import of nuclear equipment, and knowhow for power generation is not available to the country. The NSG had even frowned upon the Russian decision in the late 1990s to provide India with two VVER 1,000 MWe power plants in Koodankulam. However, Russia had then argued that the deal with India had been finalised before April 3, 1992,[4] the date when the FSS clause became operational. Hence, it was justified as not being in contravention of the NSG guidelines. But are Koodankulam 3 and 4 possible? Would the NSG allow its members such as France and China, that are keen, to indulge in nuclear trade with India?

Going strictly by the NSG guidelines, the answer to the above questions appears negative. But a few factors and certain contemporary trends might make it possible for NSG member countries to contribute to India's nuclear power programme. These may be classified under three heads: NSG-related; India-specific; and politico-technological.

NSG-Related Possibilities

Formed in 1974 as the London Club, the NSG still operates like a club and outsiders do not generally get to know its proceedings. Its decisions are taken by consensus and statements issued at the end of the meetings disclose the major outcomes. The guidelines operative today were so formulated. But certain windows of opportunity may be detected and these offer the NSG-related possibilities for India.

The first of these relates to the *status of the NSG guidelines.* For all their comprehensiveness, these, however, do not have the force or sanctity of an international treaty. Each NSG member, through requisite national legislation, voluntarily implements them. While the guidelines are adopted through consensus, they do no more than offer a set of principles that supplier nations must apply while processing applications for exports. But the actual decision on the application is taken at the national level in accordance with national export licensing requirements. Therefore, rejection of licence applications by member states is based on their individual national export controls that are expected to conform to common conditions of supply and principles voluntarily agreed to in the NSG. Unlike the case of some other multilateral arrangements such as the COCOM, where another member could veto the request for an exception to the embargo for a particular transfer, there is no such possibility in the NSG. The largely voluntary nature of the NSG guidelines applied at the national level at the discretion of the national legislature could allow a wide berth for interpretation, and national laws, if so desired, can be tailored or amended to allow for nuclear exports.

Secondly, NSG guidelines *permit islanded safeguards* or transfer of nuclear technology without FSS under two special circumstances:

(a) in the case of transfers that pertain to agreements or contracts drawn up on, or prior to, April 3, 1992; it is on this ground that the Indo-Russian Koodankulam agreement has been justified;

(b) in exceptional cases when such transfers are essential for the safe operation of existing facilities and on humanitarian grounds. Interestingly, since the NSG guidelines do not define the exceptional cases when safety considerations apply, this clause allows some room for interpretation and many exports could be explained as belonging to this category. In this context, it may also be noted that the US, despite insisting on FSS under its Nuclear Non-Prolifcration Act of 1978, acceded to India's request for some nuclear components for the two light water reactors that had been imported from General Electric in the early 1960s. President Carter, in fact, in 1980, overruled the US Nuclear Regulatory Commission's refusal to issue an export licence for fuel for Tarapur and ordered the fuel to be supplied—a decision that was sustained by a two-vote margin in the Senate.[5] He did so in the hope of extracting certain non-proliferation concessions from India, though they never materialised since New Delhi refused to accede to the nuclear Non-Proliferation Treaty (NPT). In June 1983, while the Reagan Administration did not order more fuel be sent to India,[6] fearing that Congress would refuse to sustain such a decision a second time, it did cite humanitarian reasons for exporting components[7] for the safe operation of the Tarapur plant.[8] In fact, the US tried to get Japan to export its General Electric-type nuclear components to India, but it refused and the US exported the parts itself. Even more recently, in 2000, Russia shipped low enriched uranium for the Tarapur plant on the grounds of its safe operation.[9]

Hence, the *safety clause* has been used and can still be invoked by countries desirous of exporting nuclear technologies to India. Of course, export of new reactors cannot be explained on these grounds. But, as is argued in the following paragraphs, for the environmental safety of the planet, it is imperative that nuclear power comes to contribute a greater share to India's growing energy needs. And, housing as it does a sixth of all human population, this cannot be underestimated.

India: A Unique Case

The uniqueness of India's case requires a deeper and broader understanding of the energy and developmental needs of the country and the role of nuclear power in future energy security. It is imperative to comprehend the issues that make India an exceptional case compelling that the NSG guidelines be applied in a "country-specific" framework. This would ensure that the twin goals of nuclear non-proliferation and flow of technology and materials for nuclear power for developmental purposes are fulfilled. Such a country-specific approach currently exists in the NSG framework and the extent of its application along with concurrent measures required needs discussion. While indigenous development of nuclear technology will continue to see India through, if higher targets are to be achieved within the time-frames projected by the DAE, import of newer power plants, technology and easy access to nuclear materials will assume significance. Whether the NSG will or will not concede these demands is an issue that will be analysed in the second half of this paper, but the following paragraphs flag the India-specific factors that need a country-specific approach toward India for its access to nuclear technology for peaceful developmental purposes.

Growing Economy, Energy Requirements and Environmental Concerns

History has demonstrated that economic development necessary to combat poverty and improve standards of living depends on the reliable and affordable delivery of sufficient amounts of energy. Infrastructure such as industrial enterprises and associated facilities, public transportation, schools, medical facilities, and services like sewage treatment, water supply and purification, medical treatment, and food production—almost every critical element of a sustainable economy—all require steady and sufficient supplies of electricity. Delivering energy in the most environmentally compatible and friendly manner, therefore, is the biggest challenge. As stated in the Rio Declaration 1992, the goal now is "development that meets the needs and aspirations of the present generation without compromising the ability of future generations to meet their own needs." This is a daunting task.[10]

It may be considered even more so in the case of India. Emerging as a fast-growing economy, targeting ambitious growth rates of seven to eight per cent over the next two decades, and with a growing population, an increase in India's energy consumption is inevitable.[11] With energy being the engine of economic growth and development, India will be a major consumer of energy in the coming decades.[12] The World Bank estimates place growth rate of energy demand in India at 5.3 per cent per annum in the first decade of the 21st century, and by 2020, it is expected to grow by 10 per cent per annum. This, according to International Energy Agency estimates would be met by an increase in the power generating capacity from 106 GW to 212 GW between 1996 and 2010.[13]

The steady rise in energy consumption and its generation will bring its concomitant implications. At present, coal[14] remains the dominant fuel at 55 per cent of primary energy consumption, with the share of oil consumption at 36 per cent of total energy consumption.[15] Thermal power plants have the problem of GHG emissions that cannot be wished away despite improvement in these technologies and stringent environmental measures applied at the plants. Carbon dioxide (CO_2) is the main substance associated with the greenhouse effect and global warming. Fossil fuels (coal, oil and gas) disperse CO_2 directly into the air. This pollution will naturally increase with the upsurge in energy production and will contribute to climate change and ozone depletion. To some extent, effects of this were evident in the summer of 2003 when parts of Europe suffered an unprecedented heat wave. In order to arrest further similar kinds of climate swings, environmental experts warn that the overall global CO_2 emissions should be cut from 25 billion tonnes annually to 10 billion tonnes, even as overall energy production increases.

Table 1 shows the CO_2 emissions from different energy sources in order to establish that coal, oil and gas remain major sources of carbon emissions, while nuclear and other renewable energy sources figure around the lowest.

Table 1. **Carbon Dioxide Emissions from Power Technologies in g/kWh (1)**

Coal	Advanced Coal	Oil	Gas	Nuclear	Biomass	PV	Hydro	Wind
960-1,300	800-860	690-870	460-1,230	9-100	37-166	30-150	2-410	11-75

Source: Rangan Bannerjee, "Assessment of Role of Renewable Energy Technologies," Greenhouse Gas Pollution Prevention Project-Climate Change Supplement, implemented by the Louis Berger Group Inc. Global Environment Team available at http://www.climachangeindia.com/gep_ccs/.

It is not in the scope of this paper to study the role that renewable energy technologies can play in India's energy mix, but it may be stated that these sources will not be able to generate the huge amount of energy required by the developing economy of India.

At present, India's per capita energy consumption and, hence, the resultant carbon emissions are relatively low. In fact, average per capita energy consumption in the South Asian region is the lowest in the world. In 1997/98, the average per capita energy consumption of India was less than 0.5 tonnes of oil equivalent (TOE) compared to the world average of 1.7 TOE.[16] The regional per capita electricity consumption of 219 kilowatt hours (kWh), and of India at about 400 kWh were also far below the world average of 2,258 kWh in 1997/98. As a direct consequence of this, per capita carbon emissions are also relatively low. In 1997, India emitted 250 kg of carbon per person, which was approximately one-quarter of the world average and less than 0.05 per cent of that in the US.[17]

But with continued urbanisation, a shift from non-commercial to commercial fuels, increased use of motorised vehicles, and prolonged use of older and inefficient coal-fired plants, these values are expected to increase and nearly triple by 2020. The absolute increase in emissions will partially be a function of the degree to which coal serves as a major energy source.

This trend can be effectively reversed with the increase in the use of nuclear power since this energy produces almost no emissions of CO_2 or any other GHG. In fact, today's nuclear reactors (when viewed as an alternative to coal-generated electricity) are already preventing emissions of 2.5 billion tonnes per year of CO_2—which is about half the CO_2 emitted by the world's motor vehicles.[18] Expanded use of nuclear energy could do far more. This would be most relevant in the case of India since a *resurgent economy will require increased energy* and the *demands will have to be met.* Whether this is done in an environmentally sustainable way or not shall depend on India's ability to manage its energy mix. This, meanwhile, will be determined by the kind of cost-effective and environmentally safe technologies that are available with it. But, certainly, an expansion of the Indian nuclear power programme would be beneficial not only to India, but worldwide as well.

Moreover, it also merits consideration that inclusion of uranium in the global energy portfolio would slow the depletion rate of fossil resources, sustaining the availability of energy supplies to meet future development needs. Moreover, in contrast to fossil fuels, reserves of fissionable heavy metals have no other major use. Dedicating uranium fuel to the central-station production of electricity would free fossil resources for other applications, such as residential heating and cooking, personal transportation, etc. activities for which direct use of nuclear fuels would not be appropriate.

India's de facto Status as a Nuclear Weapon State (NWS)

The uniqueness of India's position as a responsible potential member of the NSG also stems from its *de facto* status as an NWS. The NPT defines an NWS as "one which has manufactured and exploded a nuclear weapon or other explosive nuclear device prior to 1 January, 1967." Evidently, this definition does not require the acknowledged five states to physically possess nuclear weapons in order to be treated as weapon states, but merely lays down that they should have carried out a nuclear test before the designated date of January 1, 1967, and thereby divides them into weapon and non-weapon states. This definitional lacuna, however, has showed up prominently after North Korea withdrew from the NPT and declared that it possesses nuclear weapons and is building more of them, though it has not conducted any nuclear tests.

As far as the NSG is concerned, it does not specifically define a nuclear or non-nuclear state in its guidelines. Nevertheless, the guidelines are applied in a selective manner since FSS do not apply in the case of the NWS. Also, one interpretation of INFCIRC/254, Part 1 establishes that the NWS are not subject to the requirement of final use guarantees.[19] While it is understandable that the dominant powers led by the United States would not wish to acknowledge India as an NWS, leave alone accord it a *de jure* status, they are also increasingly aware of the reality that India is a *de facto* NWS and shall exist so until universal nuclear disarmament treats everyone's nuclear arsenals in a similar manner. At the same time, New Delhi has always pursued policies of restraint and responsibility in issues related to nuclear technology and weapons. Its record of non-proliferation is amongst the very best in the world. Therefore, the question is whether the NSG would take the *de facto* status/capabilities and overall responsible conduct India into account while dealing with the country and, hence, treat it differently from others.

If India were to be accepted as a country at par with the NWS for the limited purpose of requisite waivers/concessions in the NSG guidelines, then it would not have to accept FSS since this is only for transfers to a non-nuclear weapon state (NNWS). Russian diplomats have already argued that since India, by virtue of the May 1998 tests, has become a *de facto* NWS, looser controls should be applied over nuclear exports that should be allowed to it.[20]

Impeccable Record as a Nuclear Exporter

Another factor that must be highlighted is that India's nuclear exports have always been for peaceful purposes, above board, and subject to IAEA requirements. This quality of India is particularly relevant in the contemporary scenario when revelations about nuclear proliferation through a thriving black market are breaking news everyday. Iran and Libya have disclosed their ability to get weapons of mass destruction (WMD) related technology from Pakistan. In November 2003, the IAEA reported the construction of a gas centrifuge plant by the Iranian government, after Iran acknowledged the highly guarded secret. Subsequently, IAEA inspectors determined that Iran had received classified designs and components for uranium-processing gas centrifuge machines from Pakistani scientists. These complex centrifuge machines are designed to extract small amounts of fissile material from natural uranium by spinning it at supersonic speeds, and according to the IAEA, are covered with Pakistan's fingerprints. A.Q. Khan,[21] the main accused is himself believed to have stolen these from Belgian and Dutch companies in the 1970s. In the following decades, Khan studied the designs and made modifications to make the machines more stable. The centrifuge technology found in Iran recently has these modifications and capitalises on the same technology found in Khan's designs, and at times even uses old, cast-off parts from outdated Pakistani centrifuge machines. Also, the IAEA has strong evidence supporting the belief that North Korea leapfrogged many technological hurdles by buying intelligence from Pakistani scientists.

In contrast, India's record as a nuclear exporter is commendable. It has a stringent export policy in place with no likelihood of imports finding their way into the wrong hands. To further illustrate the point, Table 2 graphically details the proliferation behaviour of five countries.

As is clearly evident from Table 2, India is the only country that despite not being bound by any formal commitment to the non-proliferation regimes and export guidelines has still abided by them most diligently. In fact, recent disclosures of proliferation as have tumbled out from Iran and Libya reinforce this point even further. It is known that there are 150 Indian scientists, mostly

Table 2. **Comparative Proliferation Behaviour**

Criterion	USA	Russia	China	India	Pakistan
Use of nuclear weapons	Yes	No	No	No	No
Deployed missile-based nuclear forces in territories of other countries	Yes	Yes	Yes	No	No
Provided another country with weapons design, information, test data or computer codes hardware or special nuclear material	Yes	Yes	Yes	No	Yes
Received nuclear weapons design information, test data, hardware or special nuclear material	No	No	Yes	No	Yes
Supplied nuclear assistance to unsafeguarded facility	Yes	Yes	Yes	No	Yes
Violated non-proliferation commitments	Yes	Yes	Yes	No	Yes

retired from the Defence Research and Development Organisation (DRDO), who are working in Libya today, but the Libyan government has confirmed that none of them is involved in any sensitive areas. The Indian Embassy has kept a close tab on scientists working abroad and the basic rules of a "cooling-off" period of at least two years after leaving a government job have been diligently applied.

Given this track record and its domestic export control legislative infrastructure, there is no reason why the NSG members should not accord India with a special consideration for the supply of nuclear exports. In fact, India has even stated that it would see no serious hurdle in instituting and tightening necessary export controls to make them even more proliferation resistant. With adequate incentives in the form of NSG guidelines allowing access to nuclear technology for peaceful purposes, the institution and implementation of such controls would receive much greater and wider public support within the country.

Politico-Technological Dimensions

Certain contemporary international technological trends and political equations too make it possible for the NSG to reconsider its approach towards India. These are examined in the following sections.

Nascent Nuclear Renaissance

After a period of relative slackness in the nuclear markets in the US and Europe, there are now stirrings of a nuclear renaissance in these regions. In the US, an important study conducted by the Massachusetts Institute of Technology (MIT) has emphasised the role of nuclear power for US energy security in the coming decades.[22] Also, the *Annual Energy Outlook 2004* published by the US Department of Energy reverses its own estimate made five years ago that had predicted that by 2020 more than half the country's nuclear capacity would be closed down. Instead, the new outlook envisages a nuclear capacity increase to 103 GWe in 2025, mainly as a result of plant upgrades and a new plant in 2007.[23]

Meanwhile, in Europe too, a report prepared for the European Economic and Social Committee, which advises the European Commission, makes it clear that Europe cannot do without nuclear power. Declaring it "entirely unreasonable" to assume that renewables could do the same job in providing power without carbon emissions, the report further stated "abandoning nuclear power would be prohibitively expensive for EU consumers."[24]

Buoyed by such reports the nuclear industry in the developed countries is undertaking more R&D to tackle the issues that restrain the widespread growth of nuclear power. These include high costs of plant construction, safety issues, waste management and enhancing proliferation resistance. In order to finance these developments and to tide them through the time taken by the West to place new orders, the nuclear industry is enthused by the energy projections in Asia, and particularly in China and India. Often, proliferation concerns have reined in purely commercial deals in this field. But market forces and commercial interests have outweighed export controls in the past,[25] and they would exert greater influence in these times of globalisation and privatisation. They could compel governments to accept a certain laxity in export controls, particularly in the case of countries that do have sound non-proliferation credentials, such as India. This may be further eased by the current trend in Indo-US relations.

Improving Indo-US Relations

The thaw in bilateral relations of the two largest democracies has seen the emergence of a strategic relationship, including cooperation in areas of high technology such as space and nuclear. After his visit to the US in December 2003, Indian Prime Minister Atal Behari Vajpayee said that a "groundbreaking nuclear and high-tech pact with the United States was a milestone in bilateral ties." US President George W. Bush too promised closer links with India over nuclear regulation and safety, missile defence and civilian uses of space technology.[26] The agreement between the two has shifted requests for export of sensitive technologies to India from "presumption of denial" to "presumption of approval."[27] The two sides are also determined to tighten restrictions to try to curb the spread of WMD. There is also a convergence of interests over fighting terrorism, and India and the US are closer than ever before. In fact, even differences of opinion such as those over the US' trust in Pakistan, India's decision not to send troops to Iraq, etc. have not affected the overall constructive orientation of Indo-US relations. This trend is considerably sustained in the US by the larger comprehension that in the post-Cold War times, a solidly democratic country such as India that has a long tradition of institutional stability could be a reliable partner in meeting US interests in Asia. This perception has led to expanded economic, commercial and defence cooperation, including the conduct of a series of unprecedented joint military exercises.

Some Indian analysts, however, are still sceptical that the constructive engagement with the US would result in Washington going to the extent of amending or circumventing the NSG guidelines to help India's power programme.[28] Nevertheless, the "glide path" does hold a lot of promise. Most importantly, the initiative implies an attempt by the US to find ways of cooperating in areas that were hitherto regarded as taboo. It is most certain to result in American assistance in safety mechanisms for India's nuclear facilities, as well as greater cooperation between the nuclear regulatory agencies of the two countries. In a broader sense, it will ease unilateral licensing requirements for the transfer of high technology and dual-use items.

These developments are not of little significance. For one, they would enhance nuclear safety in India, foster a better bilateral understanding between the nuclear establishments and pave the way for greater cooperation in the future. Secondly, at another level, the initiation of US contribution to India's nuclear power programme would encourage other keen nuclear suppliers such as France and Russia, to bid for deals for their nuclear industries as well.

Asian Multi-Directional Transfers

Yet another emerging trend demands attention while analysing India's relations with the NSG. With local economic and industrial development, more and more countries, including Indonesia, Iran, Malaysia, China, Mexico, etc. are emerging as suppliers of dual-use items. Not all of them are presently members of the NSG. Considering that many of them are in Asia, the prospect for cooperation among Asian countries, particularly since the energy demand heartland shall also exist in this region in the coming years, is substantive. In fact, Asia is the only region where electricity-generating capacity from nuclear power is growing significantly. In East and Southeast Asia, there are currently 98 nuclear power reactors in operation, 22 under construction, and there are plans to build a further 39, mostly in China, Japan, South Korea and India.[29] This trend could translate into Asian cooperation in nuclear power related manufacturing, supplementing the one-way transfer of nuclear power plants and equipment from only

NSG countries with multi-directional transfers of equipment and technology among Asian countries.

India could particularly explore the option of receiving nuclear reactors from China, or even from other third countries through China. Beijing is not a member of the NSG, but has a substantial and fast expanding nuclear power programme.[30] In the wake of improving Indo-China relations, this may not be a far-fetched idea. Also it could be strengthened with other practical and economic considerations such as the financial and job benefits that could accrue to the Chinese nuclear industry through such commerce with India.

Emergence of New Concepts

In November 2003, during Prime Minister Vajpayee's visit to Moscow, Russian Atomic Energy Minister Alexander Rumyantsev reportedly offered floating nuclear plants (FNPs) to India.[31] The Russians have suggested this as one way of circumventing the NSG guidelines since, in the case of FNPs, the ownership of the plant remains with the supplier. The supplier would also provide the operational crew, security to the plant, store the radioactive waste, generate power and sell it to the country along whose coast it is stationed. The buyer would have no responsibility for, or control over, the plant, and, hence, the recipient nation may or may not accede to the condition of FSS. Therefore, Russia believes that if it were to provide India with FNPs, the NSG would not come into the picture. "We won't be breaking any NSG restrictions if we build a floating nuclear power plant and trawl it to India's shores. The plant will be operated by Russian personnel, and we'll just be selling electricity to India," Rumyantsev said.[32]

Though the concept of building a series of FNPs to meet energy requirements in Russia's remote territories is more than a decade old, the decision to offer these to other countries was not made until 2002.[33] The plant on offer is expected to be able to generate enough electricity and thermal energy to support a town of 50,000 people, or provide enough fresh water for one million people. Mounted on a barge, it could be towed to a point along India's coastline and operate for four years without reloading nuclear fuel. With a special desalination platform attached to it, the reactor would be able help desalinate sea water. Such desalination plants would have wide-ranging demand in countries with dense populations along their coastline. India, China and Indonesia are likely nations to be interested in such floating platforms.

New Dangers of Proliferation

The Pakistani proliferation scandal has amply highlighted the new dangers of WMD proliferation despite the existence of a long proclaimed "robust" non-proliferation regime. This has now been conceded by President Bush too who, in an address to the National Defence University in Washington, enunciated new initiatives aimed at damage control. Among other proposals, he called for strengthening laws and international controls, including export controls. This holds special significance for India since Bush's exhortation to the NSG to refuse to sell enrichment and reprocessing equipment to any state that does not already possess such full-scale functioning plants could prove to be an opportunity for India considering that it has the full fuel cycle capability. Could this then be interpreted as a possibility that the NSG would lift its embargoes on India?

Bush has also mandated that only states that have signed the Additional Protocol to the NPT be allowed to import equipment for their civilian nuclear programmes. This protocol requires states to declare and provide more intrusive details, and allow IAEA snap inspections over a broad range of nuclear activities and facilities. Interestingly, the US Senate itself is yet to ratify this protocol, though the US signed it in 1998. But can the protocol be signed by India without acceding to the NPT? Would the P-5 allow India to sign the protocol as a nuclear weapon state and, thus, make it eligible for importing nuclear reactors, technology and material without having to accept fullscope safeguards? Can this be one way of India being allowed entry into the non-proliferation regime and being granted nuclear weapon status?

Moreover, the foolishness in denying civilian nuclear technology to countries like India is brought out when Bush himself concedes the loophole in the NPT that was exploited by North Korea and Iran by covertly using civilian programmes to produce weapons-usable nuclear material. In fact, while the non-proliferation regime failed to catch the real proliferators, it unfairly targeted genuine non-proliferators such as India. As a way to plug the loophole, Bush has suggested that the world must create a safe, orderly system to field civilian nuclear plants without adding to the danger of proliferation by ensuring that only states that have renounced enrichment and reprocessing have reliable access at reasonable cost to fuel for civilian reactors. But it would be helpful if the NSG were to offer newer reactor technologies that are more efficient and proliferation resistant to countries that already have the enrichment and reprocessing technology overtly established but whose nuclear export policy too is above board and beyond question.

Bush has promised to include and hear out friends and allies on all new measures. India, as a strategic ally of the US, could play a meaningful role. In fact, India's national security advisor Brajesh Mishra has emphasised the need for multilateral consultative machinery with international credibility to legitimise the US measures. He categorically stated that "clubbing partners against proliferation with countries of true proliferation concern" would be a self-defeating approach. India has a unique opportunity to make the presence of its nuclear power programme and weapons status felt at this juncture.

Conclusion

In contrast to the US and most of Western Europe where growth in electricity generating capacity and particularly nuclear power appears to have levelled, for some time at least, a number of countries in Asia are planning and building new power reactors to meet their increasing demands for electricity. Projections of new generating capacity in this region envisage 56 GWe/yr up to 2020, out of which at least 39 GWe is expected to come from nuclear power, and this share could be even more if environmental constraints limit fossil fuel expansion.[34]

In India, where presently 14 units are in operation, nuclear power supplies less than 4 per cent of the electricity. However, in view of the huge demands likely, the share of nuclear would have to increase. Already six new plants are under construction and seven more are planned. While expansion plans carry on, the situation would be considerably eased if NSG members could allow nuclear exports to the country without an insistence on FSS. India would have no hesitation in accepting facility-specific safeguards, as it has done earlier in the case of Tarapur and Koodankulam.

As an emerging economic heavy, weight, a *de facto* NWS state, and a reliable nuclear exporter itself, India presents a case that must be considered as a unique one. In fact, the NSG would do well to reconsider the strict application of the FSS principle if, in turn, India would offer some major concession in non-proliferation terms without fully acceding to the NPT. If, for example, a strictly verified fissile material cut-off was to be accepted by the country, could this be a reason for the suppliers to relax supply conditions for reactor technology and fuel supply?

The international community, is today painfully aware of the global reach and lethality of terrorism. It has also been reiterated that the breeding grounds of terrorism are the economically underdeveloped and disaffected sections of the population. Therefore, for the sake of more equitable economic development, and environmental sustainability, it is imperative that unnecessary restrictions on nuclear transfer are removed. A thriving black market in weapons related knowhow and products has already proved the inability of export controls to track the movement of every nuclear related piece of information, design or material. Meanwhile, genuine cases of nuclear power expansion are suffering. It, therefore, seems the right time to consider whether it would not be more useful to apply the NSG guidelines on a more case by case basis, wherein a country like India could receive its due with little danger of promoting nuclear proliferation.

Notes

1. This point is particularly well brought out in the MIT study, "The Future of Nuclear Power: An Interdisciplinary MIT Study" (Massachusetts: MIT, 2003).
2. For more on this, see Manpreet Sethi, "Nuclear Suppliers' Guidelines: A Status Report," unpublished paper 1 in this series.
3. US, German, Canadian, Chinese and European technologies were exported through the 1970s and 1980s to many so-called "threshold states."
4. In fact, a general agreement on nuclear cooperation had been finalised on November 20, 1988, by the then Indian Prime Minister Rajiv Gandhi and Soviet leader Gorbachev, for the Soviet Union to provide India with a multi-billion dollar credit package to purchase the LWRs. The original contract called for the reactors to be provided by Soviet vendor Atomstroiexport on a turnkey basis and operated by Indian technicians trained in the Soviet Union. After years of deadlocked negotiations, Russian President Yeltsin, during a visit to India in late 1993 convinced Indian officials that the deal could be revived. However, the collapse of the Soviet Union, and subsequent difficulties in financing the project in hard currency, led to the project being put on the back-burner and a supplementary agreement was worked out on June 21, 1998, to revive the project, with the reactors to be built not on a turnkey basis as envisaged earlier, but by the Nuclear Power Corporation of India Ltd. (NPCIL) based on the Russian VVER design and engineering supervision.
5. Nuclear Control Institute, Washington, "Reagan Administration to Approve Nuclear Exports to India Despite Ban in NNPA," Press Release, June 21, 1983.
6. Instead, the Reagan Administration arranged for France to replace the United States as a supplier of fuel for the Tarapur reactors.
7. The items included pump sales and valves and other spare parts including instruments to show the intensity of neutrons produced by the chain-reacting core of each of the power plant's reactors.
8. n. 5.
9. This decision evoked strong criticism from the US and NSG. For a detailed statement, see "US Deeply Regrets Russian Shipment of Uranium Fuel to India," Washington File, US State Department, February 16, 2001.
10. Nuclear Energy Institute, "Nuclear Electricity: A Key to Sustainable Development," Public Policy Issue Brief, September 2000.

11. Tata Energy Research Institute (TERI) site, "Indian Energy Sector," updated March 2003, http://www.teriin.org/energy/Indian energy sector.htm

12. India's current oil consumption is around 83 million tonnes per year. If the GDP rate grows at an expected rate of 17 per cent (it has grown at an average annual figure of 6.6 per cent in real terms for the past nine years), the requirement will be 350-400 million tonnes per year by 2010. Jasjit Singh, "Growing South Indian Interests in the Persian Gulf Region: Problems and Opportunities," *Strategic Analysis,* vol. 23, no. 9, December 1999.

13. International Energy Agency, *World Energy Outlook* (Paris: IEA, 1998).

14. According to British Petroleum estimates, Indian coal reserves comprise 8 per cent of the world total. The country is the fourth largest producer of coal and lignite in the world (after the United States, China, and Australia). Despite India's large reserves of coal, there has been an increase in coal imports, which have grown from 6 million tonnes in 1991/92 to 20 million tonnes in 1999/2000, a rate of growth of 16 per cent a year (MoC 2001). TERI, n. 11.

15. India's import dependency for crude oil is likely to increase from 70 per cent in the 1999-2000 to 90 per cent in the coming decades. See Jasjit Singh, ed., *Oil and Gas in India's Security* (New Delhi: Knowledge World, July 2000), p. ix.

16. Amit Kumar, "Energy Scenario in South Asia," *Energy Technology News* (TERI), Issue 1, October 2000.

17. Ibid.

18. Information Brief, World Nuclear Association, http://www.world-nuclear.org

19. Point made by Carmen Richter Ribeiro Moura, Division of Disarmament and Sensitive Technologies, Ministry of External Relations, Brazil at the NSG organised International Seminar on the "Role of Export Controls in Nuclear Non-Proliferation," Vienna, October 7-8, 1997.

20. WISE (Amsterdam) News Communique, "India: Construction of Koodankulam Begins," October 19, 2001.

21. Khan, along with Mohammed Farooq, a senior scientist and high-ranking manager of Pakistan's nuclear weapons laboratory, chief nuclear engineer Dr Nazir Ahmed, as well as a number of former army officials, who were responsible for the security of the nuclear establishment are accused of trading the nation's nuclear secrets for money. Real estate holdings and millions of dollars were transferred to bank accounts controlled by the two scientists around the same time Iran was gaining its nuclear technology. For more on this see "Cold War Lingers With New Nuclear Threats," http://www.nuclearno.com, January 30, 2004.

22. n. 1.

23. "US Electricity Projections Show More Nuclear," *World Nuclear Association Weekly Digest,* January 2, 2004.

24. "EU Report Supports Nuclear Role," *Nucleonics Week,* January 29, 2004.

25. See n. 1.

26. "India Says Deeper Nuclear Ties with US Mark Key Milestone in Ties," *Agence France Press,* January 13, 2004.

27. Jyoti Malhotra, "Out of Pokharan Shadow, India, US to Sign Hi-Tech Deal," *Indian Express,* December 13, 2003.

28. J.N. Dixit, "This Subcontinental Shift," *Indian Express,* February 23, 2004.

29. World Nuclear Association, http://www.world-nuclear.org

30. Presently, China has five units in operation and six under construction. With the country's electricity demand growing at 8 per cent, China is looking towards a 20-fold increase in its nuclear capacity by 2020. World Nuclear Association, http://www.world-nuclear.org

31. Ramtanu Maitra, "Russian Floating N-Plants for India," *Asia Times Online,* December 3, 2003.

32. Ibid.

33. Even before the Russians experimented with floating nuclear power plants, the concept had been tried in the US. The MH-1 A Sturgis, a naval ship, contained a 45 MW pressurised water reactor and acted as a floating nuclear power plant. It was the first floating nuclear plant to be built (and the last one built and operated by the US Army). It provided power at the Panama Canal during the Vietnam War years, allowing more boats to pass through the canal than otherwise would have been possible. For more on this, see Ibid.

34. World Nuclear Association, http://www.world-nuclear.org

5

Future of Energy Security: The Next Three Decades

Shebonti Ray Dadwal

Introduction

Concerns regarding energy security issues seem to have come full circle as recent events impacting on global politics and security have once again brought the question of stable energy—mainly oil—supplies into focus. Hence, while the 1980s and the mid-1990s had seen countries relying more on market forces to ensure energy security issues, concerns have once again surfaced on the reliability of supplies from key energy-rich regions. These concerns have been exacerbated by the fact that energy consumption is projected to increase by 54 per cent over the next two decades, with growth expected to be the strongest in the developing countries, particularly in Asia, including China and India. In fact, according to the US Energy Information Administration's International Energy Outlook 2004, "The countries of developing Asia account for 40 per cent of the total projected increment in world energy consumption and 70 per cent of the increment for the developing world alone."

Importantly, oil is expected to remain the dominant energy source worldwide through the next two decades, with a share of 39 per cent of total energy resources, driven mainly by a robust growth in transportation, where few economically competitive alternatives have emerged. In fact, the projected increment in worldwide oil

---

Dr. Shebonti Ray Dadwal is Senior Editor, Financial Express.

use is expected to need an additional 44 million barrels a day (mbd) over current levels.

This is followed by natural gas, which is projected to increase by 67 per cent. But despite being the fastest growing source of primary energy, the projected growth in gas demand has come down over last year's forecasts due to a slower projected decline in nuclear power generation (which is its main competitor in the power sector) and concerns about the long-term ability of natural gas producers to bring sufficient resources to market at prices that are competitive with other fuels. Hence, while the demand for natural gas is expected to be more pronounced in the industrialised world and the former Soviet Union countries, in the developing world, nuclear generating capacity is expected to be high, with the greatest increase in nuclear generating capacity taking place in Asia. In fact, of the total increment in nuclear generating capacity worldwide, developing Asia is expected to account for 96 per cent, with 40,000 MW alone coming from China, South Korea and India.

Today, the main issues in the realm of energy are:

- Geopolitics.
- Price.
- Environmental issues.

Geopolitics

The debate over the availability of oil (and to a lesser extent gas) continues with both sides almost equally divided about the reserves situation. While several experts are of the view that there are sufficient reserves of oil to satisfy demand over the foreseeable future, there are others who say that the major oil finds have all been discovered and that production, including from the giant fields of West Asia, has peaked and is now only a few years from decline. Part of this debate arises from the lack of transparency about the reserves situation in several West Asian countries, particularly Saudi Arabia.

However, what is definitely known is that any low cost production from non-Organisation of Petroleum Exporting Countries (OPEC) sources, barring perhaps Russia, is on the decline and no new major discoveries have been made in recent years; nor are any likely to be made *that would be comparable with those in West Asia,* which has the largest known reserves of oil in the world. Of course, there has been rapid technological progress which allows the further exploitation of known sources, particularly in offshore and deep sea blocks, as well as tar sands that will allow output to rise for another decade or so. But given the high costs needed to develop these resources, they will have a bearing on prices, which will be discussed in the following section.

That geopolitics does, and probably will continue to, play an important role in energy security is clear from the fact that given the instability and political turmoil that has almost become inherent in the West Asian region, most consuming countries are looking at diversification of sources as a major part of their energy security policies. Despite assurances from Gulf suppliers on reliable supplies, the hunt for non-Gulf oil is increasing. Those who expected big economic and energy benefits from the Iraq War have been disappointed. The quagmire that the US finds itself in Iraq and the likelihood of the Israeli-Palestinian conflict continuing indefinitely have kept the issue of security of supplies alive.

The same goes for natural gas. Other than Russia, the world's major gas reserves are located in the Persian Gulf region, and the same geopolitical issues as those pertaining to oil are applicable for gas supplies. Moreover, transportation of gas through pipelines in terms of secure routes also makes it a more difficult energy resource to access.

Price

The second issue, and probably the most important one today, is the price of oil—and gas. There is no doubt that the price of energy is perhaps *the* most important factor determining a nation's choice of fuel, which includes transport and storage. In fact, it is because oil is the most cost-effective fuel, in terms of production as well as transportation and storage, that it continues to be the fuel of choice for most nations.

However, since 1999, the price of oil has been increasing steadily, due to a number of political and economic reasons, such as fear of production cuts by OPEC, political tensions in Venezuela and low US strategic inventories. So much so, that today, oil prices, which have risen by more than $10 a barrel over the last three years, are ruling at their highest witnessed over the last 13 years. In fact, several experts say that the days of cheap oil may be over. If prices are ruling high due to the depletion of conventional or low cost oil reserves as mentioned above, then that is understandable. However, there is another school of thought which believes that there are enough reserves to last for the next 40-50, even 100 years, and the price hike is due to other reasons.

One reason, of course, is that the US-led operation in Iraq did not work out as expected. The continuing violence in that country, including the sabotaging of export pipelines and the delay in reconstructing the moribund oil sector has prevented the production and export of Iraqi oil as was expected.

Secondly, the prospects of terrorist attacks on Saudi oil installations and the increasing spread of Islamic radicalism throughout the West Asian region have led to speculation on the security of supplies, which in turn has a bearing on prices.

But more importantly, the manipulation of the market by cutting production to set prices at levels suited to the producers has led to volatility in oil prices.[1] Recently, some OPEC members have voiced their preference for hiking the price bandwidth of their crude basket from the earlier $22-28 per barrel by around 30 per cent. A major reason for this is the knowledge that the OPEC members are sitting comfortably on the majority of the world's reserves, and are the only major providers of any increase in demand.

During the late 1990s, and again in 2002-03, oil demand worldwide dropped as a result of economic recession, first in the Asia-Pacific countries and then in the US and other developed countries. But over the last few months, with the onset of economic recovery in the US, demand has and is expected to, increase further. Moreover, according to the International Energy Agency (IEA), world demand is increasingly being spurred by burgeoning demand in the developing countries, particularly India and China.

Any sharp increase in oil price has an adverse impact on the global economy. According to a May 2004 IEA report, world Gross Domestic Product (GDP) growth could have been higher by at least half a percentage point in the last two to three years had prices remained at mid-2001 levels.

While high oil prices impact adversely on all countries, those countries which have a higher dependency on imports and have oil intensive economies are affected more severely. Hence, the adverse economic impact of higher oil prices on oil-importing developing countries is more severe than on the developed countries, because their economies are more dependent on imported oil and are more energy-intensive as they tend to use energy less efficiency. They are also less able to weather financial turmoil brought about by higher oil import costs.

China is believed to have accounted for 37 per cent of the growth in world oil consumption over the last four years, much of which was imported, while India's dependence on oil imports, currently at 70 per cent, is expected to increase to around 90 per cent over the next two decades. In fact, India spent about $15 billion (3 per cent of its GDP) on oil imports in 2003, which is 16 per cent higher than its 2001 oil import bill.

Hence, with oil prices showing little tendency of loosening in the near future, or even over the next couple of years, if at all, developing countries like India will be adversely affected unless they can reduce their dependence on imported oil by finding alternative sources of energy.

Environmental Issues

International concern over rising atmospheric concentrations of greenhouse gases (GHG), of which carbon dioxide (CO_2) was identified as the largest contributor, and their possible adverse effects on the global climate system resulted in the adoption of the United Nations Framework Convention on Climate Change (UNFCCC) in 1992. More importantly, one of the two major anthropogenic sources of CO_2 emissions was identified as the combustion of fossil fuels (land-use changes, especially deforestation, was the other). As a result, environmental concerns may very well emerge as the single most important factor that will decide the fate of various fuels over the coming decades.

Much of the projected increase in CO_2 emissions is expected to come from the industrialising world, mainly because of the large increases in energy use as many of these countries' economies grow at a brisk pace. In fact, the developing countries are believed to account for 61 per cent of the projected increment in CO_2 emissions between 2001 and 2025 because of the increased use of fossil fuels, both for the power sector (coal and natural gas) as well as in the transport sector.[2] This is exacerbated because unlike in the industrialised countries which have succeeded in reducing their levels of energy intensity, the developing countries still maintain a high level of the same, despite some improvement in recent years.

It is now a well established fact that amongst all the fuels, both conventional and non-conventional, nuclear energy is the only energy source that produces virtually no GHG emissions. According to the World Nuclear Association estimates, each year nuclear power plants around the world avoid emissions up to 2.5 billion tonnes of CO_2. According to International Atomic Energy Agency (IAEA) estimates, emissions from the entire nuclear fuel cycle—from uranium mining to waste disposal—are in the range of 10-15 g of CO_2/kWh, which is of the same order as emissions from wind energy. Compare this with emissions from the use of fossil fuels, which range from 450-1200 g/CO_2/kWh.

According to the Special Report on Emissions Scenarios of the Intergovernmental Panel on Climate Change (IPCC) in 2002, the potential of nuclear energy to mitigate climate change will remain a notable part of the energy-mix irrespective of the different policies and scenarios evolved to reduce GHG emissions.

Given these facts, it is, therefore, ironical that nuclear power figures only marginally in the UNFCCC negotiations. In fact, the Kyoto Protocol restricts the use of nuclear energy as a means to achieve emissions reduction targets by Annex I parties to the Convention, and the Bonn Agreement on the protocol arrived at in July 2001, forbids the use of nuclear energy under the flexibility mechanism of joint initiatives (JI) and clean development mechanisms (CDM). A country is free to declare that a nuclear energy project would contribute to its sustainable development, although there are no certified emissions credits to be gained from the same. At an event organised during the eighth Conference of Parties (COP8), sponsored by the Organisation of Economic Cooperation and Development's (OECD's) Nuclear Energy Division, it was said that in the short and medium term, drastic GHG reductions were not possible without recourse to nuclear energy, and the foreclosing of the nuclear option runs counter to the concept of sustainable development.

As more and more countries adopt energy policies which are geared towards less dependence on imports as well as opting for fuels that are consistent with their environmental goals, the impact on the energy industry as a whole and the oil industry in particular will be substantial. Even if the 1997 Kyoto Protocol does not get implemented, the increased awareness about the climate change issues and the related impact on the environment will cause many countries to implement policies, including environment/carbon taxes, which will in time render fossil fuels, particularly oil and coal, uncompetitive vis-à-vis other energy resources.

Ironically, though nuclear energy has been identified as the energy resource which has the best emission record (almost zero), it had met with stiff resistance from some industrialised countries, including the US, mainly for political reasons. However, with GHG emissions and climate change concerns gaining precedence, there is a growing tendency, albeit gradual, among several countries, particularly the industrialising ones, to look more favourably at nuclear energy. In fact, with the danger of global climate change, the case for expanding the use of emission-free nuclear power has become more compelling. There is a growing consensus among energy experts that any effort to limit GHG emissions will require the use of more energy-efficient technologies and every non-emitting energy source—solar, wind, hydro and geothermal, and nuclear energy. Even in Europe, a report prepared for the European Economic and Social Commission makes clear that Europe cannot do without nuclear power; it says that it is unreasonable to expect renewables to do the same job in providing power without carbon emissions.

Moreover, European signatories to the Kyoto Protocol realise that it will be impossible to insulate energy from global recession while also cutting emissions. Even with lacklustre growth, Europe has missed its emissions targets, and at current rates is expected to bring emissions down by just 4.7 per cent by the time the targets become binding, compared with the 8 per cent reduction from the 1990 levels that it promised.[3]

Today, even the Bush Administration says nuclear power will be part of the country's energy future. Nuclear power already provides 20 per cent of the US' electricity. Although five years ago, it was projected that more than half the US' nuclear capacity would be closed down by 2020, the Department of Energy's (DoE) 2004 Annual Energy Outlook says that new figures show a slight increase in capacity due to plant uprates and a new start-up in 2007. In fact, the DoE's financial year 2005 budget, which reflects the US' priorities with regard to energy, mentions ensuring that nuclear power remains a key energy resource.

Although concerns about responsible management of additional nuclear waste that would be generated beyond what is currently generated continue, it is important to remember that nearly half a century of experience with nuclear energy has not diminished its capability. Many who question the value of nuclear power forget that over this period, it has become an abundant source of energy with 435 nuclear plants providing 17 per cent of the world's energy. Besides the US, other countries make even greater use of nuclear energy: France–77 per cent, Sweden–44 per cent, Switzerland–39 per cent, Japan–28 per cent and the UK–23 per cent. The IAEA has listed more than 30 nuclear power plants under construction, albeit mostly in Asia. The Bush Administration wants to explore new technology to recycle nuclear fuel, increasing its efficiency and possibly reducing its danger. Also, supporters of nuclear power say reactors are getting safer, reducing the chances of accidents.

Energy-deficient Asia is spending billions of dollars to build nuclear power plants, sparking fierce competition among global equipment makers for the bonanza. With 18 of the world's 31 units under construction located in Asia, it is dubbed by some as a renaissance of the sector and has become a massive magnet for European, Canadian and Russian suppliers. Even the US is expected to relax its curbs on the sensitive technology transfer to select Asian nations. Today, nuclear fuel makes up 1.4-3.7 per cent of the power output in Asia's two most populous nations, below 35-40 per cent for Japan and South Korea, and 78 per cent for France. Few projects have broken ground in the West in the past few years as environmental, health and security concerns have persisted since the Chernobyl accident in 1986. A growing number of ageing nuclear plants in Europe are reaching their expiry dates and it has not been decided whether they would be replaced.

To clinch the lucrative contracts in Asia, nuclear equipment suppliers have focussed on the safety records as well as competitive investment and production costs, according to analysts. Suppliers also have to convince their own governments to let them export such sensitive technologies. The governments must also build good ties to win such deals, industry experts say.[4]

The Indian Question

With a population of more than one billion and a GDP growth rate averaging around 6-7 per cent per annum over the last decade, the development aspirations of the people can only be sustained with a concurrent growth in the availability of energy. Currently, commercial energy demand in India is growing at above 6 per cent per annum, and this is expected to increase to around 10 per cent per annum over the next decade, thereby calling for an increase in power generation that is 12 times the generation in 2001-02. As a result, it is only to be expected that the energy mix will shift towards commercial energy resources from the earlier traditional or non-commercial sources.

Given this situation, one should examine the current energy resources situation in India.

The two sectors that are currently the largest consumers of energy are power (for both industry and agriculture) and transport. For the power sector, commercial sources of energy include coal, oil, natural gas, hydropower and nuclear energy, which together account for around 60 per cent of the country's energy supplies. Wood and biomass account for the rest.

Among the commercial sources, coal has a 52 per cent share while oil and gas account for around 44 per cent. Hydropower has a share of 2 per cent while nuclear energy contributes 1.7 per cent.[5]

This has led to a rapid rise in energy emissions intensity, which in turn will enhance India's share in global emissions in the next few decades. What is alarming here is that despite the rise in global emissions in India—which in 1997 alone was around 300 million tonnes of carbon equivalent—the per capita GHG emissions from India are below a quarter of the global average. This is due to rising use of coal in the power and industry sectors, as well as emission of methane from the livestock sector.[6]

Although there is a rapid rise in the use of gas in the power sector, any incremental growth in the use of natural gas will be dependent on pricing. In the meantime, oil is likely to continue to dominate the transport sector. However, since India does not have sufficient reserves of hydrocarbons, imports are expected to continue to rise. This in turn will have an impact on India's import bill, as has been mentioned in the previous section.

Moreover, around 67 per cent of India's oil supplies are sourced from the Gulf. This has security implications, given the volatile political situation in that region. Concerned about its growing reliance on the Gulf for its energy, like other major oil-importing countries, India too is seeking to diversify its energy sources from other regions. At the same time, Indian firms are investing in overseas oil and gas fields. Till date, around \$3 billion has been invested in buying equity in overseas energy blocks, which include Russia (Sakhalin), North and West Africa (Sudan and Algeria), Myanmar, Vietnam and Syria, and India is currently negotiating with Iran for the same. India is expecting to have access to around 20 million tonnes of equity oil by 2020.

The previous National Democratic Alliance (NDA) government had also taken a decision to set up strategic petroleum reserves (SPR), which could be tapped in times of supply shortfalls as well during extreme price volatility. However, due to the high cost of setting up and maintaining SPRs, India is currently looking at setting up a 15 million tonne SPR to begin with, which could be increased over time to allow it to have access to around 45 days worth of crude supplies.

However, while all these strategies will enhance India's energy security to some extent, with its demand for energy growing exponentially, India will continue to remain dependent on oil and gas imports. On the other hand, India has world-class expertise and self-reliance in all areas and activities related to nuclear power generation. It not only prospects, mines and mills its own uranium, converts it into yellowcake, produces heavy water, manufactures reactor vessels, seamless calandria tubes, turbines, generators and other critical equipment, fabricates instrumentation and control systems for reactors, it also designs, builds, and operates its pressurised heavy water reactors (PWHRs), recovers plutonium as fresh fuel for use in breeder reactors and safely disposes of the radioactive wastes. It can further decommission aged reactors or extend their lives. In other words, the Indian nuclear industry has mastered a host of highly complex technologies, which no country would share with India.

One of the major criticisms directed against the use of nuclear energy is that it is far more costly compared to other fuels, particularly coal and gas. However, a French government study compares the cost of electricity from gas, coal and nuclear power between 2007-15, factoring in the costs of limiting carbon emissions. According to it, "The cost of nuclear production is more stable than that of coal and much more than that of gas."[7] Also, the vendor prices of new nuclear power plants are falling.

Besides the price factor, the other real hurdle to increasing India's nuclear power generation is the denial of technology and capital under the guise of non-proliferation, on the one hand, and lack of information and knowledge at the ground level, on the other. Therefore, public understanding and support are necessary for a successful implementation of policy.

Conclusion

With the developed countries cutting down on their use of oil in favour of natural gas sources mainly from Russia, the main (and growing) consumers of West Asian energy resources (both oil and natural gas) are, and will continue to be, the industrialising countries of Asia, particularly China and India. Between 1990 and 1997, the demand for oil in the Asia-Pacific region grew by more than 6 mbd, accounting for around 82 per cent of total oil demand growth.[8] However, as the region's indigenous resources can in no way meet this demand, the issue of locating and ensuring stable supplies to sustain their growth levels will become an important aspect of these countries' policies.

Since the West Asian producers are the only sources of supply which are in a position to meet the Asia-Pacific region's burgeoning energy demand, it is only natural that these two regions will become interdependent (for supplies and markets). However, this is also a cause of intense concern for the Western powers, particularly the US, as potential political and strategic linkages between some West Asian countries that are perceived as having interests that are inimical to Western interests, and South and East Asian countries are seen as undesirable.

Though it is generally perceived that the level of interdependence between these future producers and consumers will increase, once the sources of supply become restricted to a few producers, consumers will be more vulnerable to competition over scarce resources, disruptions of supply as well price manipulations resorted to by some of the producers. Therefore, it would be in the interest of these countries to diversify not only their sources of supply but also look at different fuels for their energy needs.

As global concerns becomes more focussed on the linkages between energy and its effect on the environment, or more particularly between the burning of fossil fuels and carbon emissions, more governments are being pressured by interest groups to look at alternative and safer energy resources, such as natural gas, hydroelectricity, solar and wind energy, and nuclear power. However, mainly due to the increase in the use of oil in almost all sectors of the economy in industrialising countries, oil is expected to retain (though not increase) its share of around 40 per cent of total world energy consumption for the next two decades. In the industrialised countries, oil will be replaced with natural gas in the power sectors,[9] due to their proximity to supply sources in Russia (Europe) and Canada (USA). However, the Asia-Pacific countries have not been able to make the transition very successfully, though liquefied natural gas (LNG) consumption has shot up in East Asia. As a result, for the less affluent countries of Asia, oil and coal (mainly in China and India) are, and will continue to be, the main energy sources, as alternative sources of energy such as solar and wind energy are unlikely to become commercially viable in the near future.

As climate change and carbon emissions become major environmental concerns, the earlier bias against nuclear energy is showing signs of dissipating, as many nations are finding that viable alternatives to nuclear power are more difficult to develop than anticipated. As a result, Finland, France, Japan (despite Tokaimura in 1999), Canada and Mexico are all expected to maintain or expand their current levels of nuclear generation capacity, while prospects for nuclear energy growth in the United States are also expected to improve following the granting of operational extensions in 2000 of 20 years each to two nuclear reactors in the country by the Nuclear Regulatory Commission. Other US companies have also requested for plant life extensions.[10]

However, the greatest incremental growth to nuclear energy is expected to come from the industrialising Asian countries like China, India and South Korea, as part of their policies to look at nuclear energy as an alternative to imported hydrocarbons, while at the same time, allowing them to keep their emissions under control. In fact, the developing world is expected to more than double its nuclear generation capacity by 2020 from 6 per cent of the world's nuclear electricity generation in 1999 to about 17 per cent by 2020, with growth coming mainly from China, South Korea and India, respectively.

As supply security, price and environmental factors begin to impact on energy issues and more importantly on their individual economies, more and more countries are abandoning their hitherto complacent attitudes to energy. While strategic reserves of hydrocarbons can stave off disruptions in supply for a while, in the event of a prolonged disruption, the energy market, which currently revolves around oil, will collapse, sending the international economy into a tailspin. As a result, more comprehensive and interdependent (amongst suppliers and consumers) policies have to be forged, whether it involves energy resources or technology, to ensure sustained availability of all kinds of energy. Currently, the Western industrialised countries have an edge over the rest of the world in new energy-related technology, whether it relates to production and extraction of unconventional oil and clean coal technology or development of alternative energy sources, including nuclear energy. Unless this technology is made accessible, the world could well be headed towards an era of future conflict over supplies, rampant and dangerous proliferation and global warming.

Notes

1. "World Oil Markets", *International Energy Outlook 2001* Report, www.iea.doe.gov/oiaf/ieo/oil.html
2. Energy Information Administration, *International Energy Outlook, 2004.*
3. "Global Warming Glasnost," *Wall Street Journal,* December 4, 2003.
4. *Business Standard,* April 12, 2004.
5. *Business Standard,* May 8, 2004.
6. "Future Energy Trends and GHG," in P.R. Shukla, Debyani Ghosh and Amit Garg, *India and Global Climate Change* (Oxford, 2004).
7. NucNet News No. 333/03, www.industrie. Gouv, fr as quoted in *WNA Newsletter,* January/February 2004.
8. Fereidun Fesharaki, "Energy and the Asian Security Nexus," *Journal of International Affairs,* Vol. 53, No. 1, Fall 1999, www.asiamedia.ucla.edu/ Deadline/Energy Needs/Articles/Fesharak.htm
9. Highlights of the *International Energy Outlook Report 2001,* at <www.iea.doe.gov/oiaf/ieo/index.html>
10. "Nuclear Power," *International Energy Outlook 2001* Report, <www.iea.doe.gov/oiaf/ieo/nuclear.html>

6

From Stasis to Revival: Trends in Nuclear Power

Jasjit Singh

> Commercial nuclear applications are invaluable in our daily lives, with thousands of industrial, agricultural, and medical applications. None, however, are more visible than the nuclear energy industry………Nuclear Power is safe, economical, reliable, and emission free.
>
> — Donald C. Hintz[1]

International Atomic Energy Agency (IAEA) Director General El Baradei recently stated, "The more we look at the future, the more we can expect countries to be considering the potential benefits that expanding nuclear power has to offer for the global environment and for economic growth."[2] He went on to emphasise that nuclear plants are most attractive where energy demand is growing and alternative resources are scarce, and where energy security and reduced air pollution and greenhouse gases are a priority. This is quite a change from only a few years ago when the international community was insisting that nuclear power should be scaled back and its production even terminated. Historically, after the initial high expectations, symbolised by President Eisenhower's "Atoms for Peace" plan of 1953 about the role that nuclear technology would play for peaceful purposes in general, and electricity generation in particular, actual progress in the expansion of nuclear

Air Commodore (Retd.) Jasjit Singh is Director, Centre for Strategic and International Studies, New Delhi.

technology for peaceful purposes slowed down perceptibly during the past quarter century. There are a number of reasons for the resultant hiatus which is beginning to give way to a renaissance and revival of nuclear power in the world, even if the shift has not received the attention it deserves.

The Three Mile Island accident in a nuclear power reactor in March 1979 and the Chernobyl accident in 1986 had a profound impression on public perceptions about the safety of nuclear plants. The negative impact of the latter accident received much higher focus partly because of the Cold War politics and ideological confrontation between the Western and Eastern blocs. Since the capital costs of a nuclear power station are substantively higher than those run from other types of fuel, the need for high investments became another factor discouraging the growth of nuclear energy. At the same time, as the dominant powers moved to curb the acquisition of nuclear science and technology in the name of non-proliferation through arms control measures that safeguarded the capabilities of the five nuclear weapon states and nuclear science and technology in the industrialised developed countries, major barriers were created for the development and expansion of nuclear technology and power for peaceful purposes. The developing countries were the most badly hit. The nuclear Non-Proliferation Treaty (NPT) even now symbolises the denial regimes it spawned and is a powerful instrument even for constricting human development that has nothing to do with nuclear weapons proliferation in spite of the fact that Article IV of the treaty essentially codified the promise of "Atoms for Peace" without which the requisite support for the NPT in the broad community may not have materialised.

There was a flurry of activities leading to rapid expansion of nuclear power in the developed countries after the 1973 oil shock which brought home the vulnerability of oil importing states like France and Japan. But as nuclear power generation stabilised and oil prices came under increasing influence of market forces and mechanisms, further expansion of nuclear power plants started to plateau in the developed states. This was further reinforced by stabilised economic growth rates and low population increases among these countries and the emphasis shifted to increasing efficiency of energy productivity and utilisation to allow conservation to compensate for the need to build larger capacity.

All this has been changing quietly. The world now operates 442 commercial power reactors (in 30 states) and 280 research reactors (in 56 states), besides 150 ships (mostly military) with 200 nuclear reactors. The world has accumulated experience of 11,000 reactor years in the civil arena; besides, the experience related to military purposes is also great. For example, the US Navy alone accumulated 5,400 reactor years experience on its warships and submarines. The initial capital investments in nuclear power plants remain high; but the economic cost of electricity generation is now lower than most other forms of electricity generation. Economic growth in the developing countries and their rising populations are demanding higher availability of electric power for domestic, commercial and industrial usage. The case of China and India is symptomatic. Climate change and global warming concerns have brought home the need for sustainable development and, hence, emphasis on nuclear power.

Fig. 1. **World Electricity Generation**

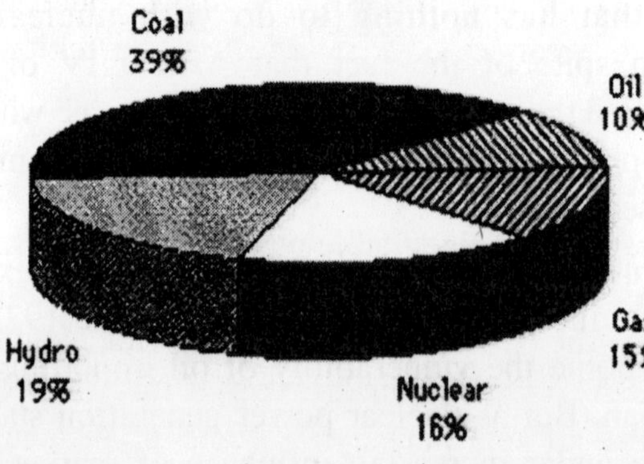

Nuclear power accounts for 16 per cent of the global electricity generation, producing 2,574 billion kilowatt hours (kWh). The United States, with 104 plants, has the most operating reactors. Lithuania has the highest proportion of electric power generated by nuclear reactors in the world with 80 per cent of its electricity from nuclear power, with France at the second place with 78 per cent of its electricity coming from nuclear plants. The developing world operates a mere 39 out of the 442 reactors. But the bulk of the new power plants now under construction are in the developing world, mostly in Asia, where 22 of the 31 new nuclear plants in recent years were located. Some Western countries like Germany, Belgium and Sweden plan to phase out their nuclear plants, although others plan to revive nuclear power. In North America, licence extensions for another 20 years of operations have already been either approved or applied for in the case of 75 per cent of US nuclear plants besides a number of plants already shut down being brought back on line in both the United States and Canada.

With the current plans to build new reactors, including those proposed to be built, nuclear power generation would increase substantively in the foreseeable future. More than 30 power reactors are under construction worldwide, equivalent to 7 per cent of existing capacity, while a similar number are firmly planned, equivalent to 10 per cent of present capacity. Most reactors under construction are located in Asia, the "energy demand heartland" of the 21st century. The current status of nuclear power reactors under operation and construction in some selected countries, especially in Asia, reveals clear signs of revival and the regions where this revival is centred, are indicated in Table 1.

Nuclear Power Trends

While there would be inevitable variations in estimating future trends, the base line adopted for global trends by the joint study undertaken by the International Institute for Applied Systems Analysis (IIASA) and the World Energy Council (WEC) is useful for the purpose of our enquiry. In case of a scenario of high economic growth through the 21st century, primary energy needs

Table 1. **Nuclear Power Reactors in Selected Countries**

	Operable	Under Construction	Planned	Proposed	Total
Japan	39	3	13	-	55
India	14	9	-	24	47
Russia	30	6	-	8	44
China (PRC)	9	2	4	22	37
South Korea	19	1	8	-	28
USA	103	1	-	-	104
France	59	-	-	-	59
UK	27	-	-	-	27

Source: *World Nuclear Power Reactors 2002-04,* Uranium Information Centre Ltd., Melbourne, March 25, 2004.

would grow at an average of 1.9 per cent per year for the first half century, dropping to 1.5 per cent during the second half. In a comparatively shorter time span, say till 2020, these forecasts are similar to those carried out by a number of organisations like the International Energy Agency (IEA), and Petroleum Economist Ltd. These trends may be summed up as follows:

- The developing world Gross Domestic Product (GDP) would grow faster than that of the developed countries.
- Worldwide primary energy would grow at 2.1 per cent per year (2000-2020) versus the growth rate of 1.7 per cent during the two decades of 1980-2000. Primary fuel patterns would remain similar to past trends with the exception that natural gas demand accelerates.
- Carbon emissions continue to rise with developing countries emissions equalling the industrialised world's emissions around 2010.
- Nuclear energy is expected to grow slowly during this period at around 1 per cent per annum.
- Electricity production grows at 2.5 per cent a year, outpacing

primary energy growth of 2.1 per cent a year, with growth in the developing world about three times that in the industrialised world.

- Developing countries' total consumption of primary energy surpasses that in the industrialised countries by 2020 as a consequence of faster economic growth and rising populations.
- There will be acceleration in the development of networks and in the transportation of fuels between countries. Electricity grids and natural gas pipeline networks would multiply. Oil transportation flows grow by 80 per cent between 1995 and 2020 owing to demand in the developing countries, besides expansion of liquefied natural gas (LNG) shipments. Increasingly, energy would be delivered by dedicated transport systems such as pipelines and networks besides other high-quality carriers. Crude oil transiting through the Strait of Hormuz is expected to increase from the earlier 49 per cent of the global transportation to as much as 55 per cent by 2020. Development of ports on Pakistan's Makran coast, especially with Chinese assistance at Gwadar, would have strategic implications for oil (and natural gas) transportation by sea.
- In the longer-term perspective, there would be an increased reliance on nuclear energy worldwide, with its share rising from the current figure of 16 per cent to roughly 40-70 per cent by the end of the 21st century.

There are realities about international geopolitical energy issues that need to be kept in mind. To start with, less than a quarter of the world's population is consuming three-quarters of the world's primary energy produced. One-third of the population of the world does not have access to electricity. On the other hand, empirical studies indicate that there is a strong correlation between energy consumption per person and the index of human development, indicating that access to energy and economic growth must translate into a legitimate right to life.

Asian Scene

High economic growth in Asia, especially the two Asian giants, China and India, who with their 2.2 billion people also account for over one-third of global population, with India's population (and, hence, increasing demand of energy simply on this ground not to talk of economic growth) continuing to grow in the future, would raise the demand for energy substantively in the coming decades. Asia's primary energy demand is expected to rise from 25 per cent of global demand in 2000 to 35-40 per cent in 2050, resulting in the focus of world energy trade shifting to Asia from the Atlantic, especially since the bulk of the hydrocarbon resources of the world are located in the Asian region. World energy markets are likely to become more independent over the longer term, with dependence on the Persian Gulf, Central Asia and Russia increasing, requiring greater international political-economic cooperation. On the other hand, the Persian Gulf-Central Asia-former Soviet territories, and Russia are likely to remain regions of instability in the foreseeable future, raising serious dilemmas for energy security of countries like India.

Both China and India rely extensively on the use of coal in their energy policies, and would have to become successful at achieving long-term sustainable development to obtain economic and political stability. In many ways, therefore, energy demand in China and India, and the way they evolve solutions to the challenges of energy requirements, would have a profound influence not only on their national scenes but also in the broader picture affecting the developing world and in turn the global scenarios. India's per capita energy consumption is half that of China, while its current emissions of carbon are less than one-third those of China and are projected to increase more slowly than China's.

While energy structures would vary greatly between sub-regions, some broad trends across all of them may be noted:

- Oil and natural gas consumption would rise for the next 30-70 years before starting to decline. Energy deficient countries like India would import increasing volumes of hydrocarbon fuels to meet their energy requirements with intrinsic dependencies and potential vulnerabilities. In economic-trade terms, substantive export earning may simply be absorbed by the outflows for importing energy with implications for import of technology and capital for industrialisation and economic growth.

- The region's heavy reliance on coal (about 70 per cent of India's coal production is used in electric power generation, the transportation of which comprises nearly 51 per cent of the massive railway network's goods traffic), and increasingly on oil, would continue to cause the region's carbon emissions to contribute between 30-35 per cent of the world's total CO_2 emissions between 2020-50.
- Nuclear and renewable energy would be evident throughout the area by 2020, would be substantial by 2050, and would meet over 50 per cent of the total energy demand by the end of the century.
- Energy infrastructure in power plants, networks, pipelines and outlets would require massive investments. Institutional reforms would be essential to encourage economic development of the energy sector.

Availability of Fossil Fuel in the Future?

Current projections indicate that use of fossil fuel will account for more than 80 per cent of the total worldwide primary energy consumption by 2010. But concerns about the future availability and access to fossil fuels, and consequent impact on energy security of nations are driving efforts to seek alternatives to fossil fuels. Nuclear energy provides an obvious alternative, especially for fossil fuel importing countries. For example, concerns about energy security led France and Japan in the early 1970s to implement an energy programme heavily in favour of nuclear energy.

Revival of Nuclear Power

A number of developments across the world indicate an emerging revival of nuclear power after a hiatus of more than two decades:

- The European Commission recently reaffirmed the need to continue—and possibly augment—reliance on nuclear energy to limit greenhouse gas emissions.
- Finland is in the final stages of acquiring a fifth nuclear power plant. In 2003, the nuclear option was confirmed by 66 per cent of the voters in Switzerland.
- Sweden, which decided in 1980 to phase out nuclear energy, now appears much more amenable to nuclear power and is likely to restart its nuclear programme.
- In Asia, Japan, India, China and South Korea all possess robust programmes, and a number of countries (especially the United States) are considering the renewal of their nuclear plants as they develop mid-term energy policies.

Nuclear energy, which has made major strides in performance, safety and costs over the past decade, is undergoing a 'rebirth' in the context of sustainable development:

- Worldwide, there are 442 nuclear reactors in 30 countries, representing a 16 per cent contribution to worldwide electricity production with an extremely wide distribution ranging from one per cent for China to over 78 per cent for France.
- As a rule, the nuclear industry has achieved a maturity due to accumulated reactor operating experience and its success, particularly in recent years, in improving performance in terms of reliability, productivity and safety factors. France, for example, has 58 nuclear reactors in 19 sites adopting the global fuel cycle management based on the reprocessing of spent fuel, separating reusable content (96 per cent) from true nuclear waste (4 per cent), recycling the recovered plutonium as fuel in 900 megawatt (MW) reactors.

- The nuclear industry (including in India) registered remarkable gains in the capacity factor, reaching 90 per cent in 2002, a 30 per cent increase from the earlier levels. This had allowed for a record generation of 778 billion kWh in 2002.

Economics of Nuclear Power

Conventional wisdom would have us believe that nuclear power is expensive compared to other forms of energy. However, recent empirical studies have indicated the reverse since the cost of nuclear power generation has been dropping over the past decade. Calculation of economic costs of energy production can be based on direct cost or they can also include what have come to be known as the "external costs." External costs are defined as those that are actually incurred in relation to health and the environment and are quantifiable but normally not included in the cost of electricity. The implications are enormous since the inclusion of external costs would double the European Union (EU) price of electricity from coal, and that from gas would increase by 30 per cent even if the costs related to the global warming factor are not included!

For nuclear power plants, the major component of cost is the capital investment which (at around 60 per cent of the plant cost as against 15 per cent for gas plant cost) is much higher than that of constructing thermal or other power plants though fuel costs in non-nuclear power generation are higher as recurring costs. Because of the high capital costs for plant construction, nuclear plants would generate greater employment opportunities and lead to a much higher level of domestic investment of financial resources as compared to import of hydrocarbon fuels by energy deficient countries like India.

Any cost figure for nuclear power plants normally includes spent fuel management, plant decommissioning and final waste disposal. These costs, while external for other technologies, are internal for nuclear power. Decommissioning costs are normally estimated at around 9-15 per cent of the initial capital cost which over time would amount to a few per cent of the cost of electricity produced. Spent fuel disposal contributes up to another 10 per cent to the overall cost per kWh. For example, the $18 billion US spent fuel programme is funded by a 0.1 cent/kWh levy.

Estimates of costs vary greatly depending upon the area/country and parameters that are taken into account. But what is common to practically all cost estimates is that nuclear energy is not only cost competitive but provides the most economic option for generation of electricity. The cost advantage of nuclear power goes up even further if external costs are applied to all forms of electricity generation. The European Commission had launched a path breaking study in 1991 "to put financial figures against damage resulting from different forms of electricity production for the entire EU." With nuclear energy, the risk of accidents was factored in along with high estimates of radiological impacts from mine tailings (waste management and decommissioning being already within the cost to the consumer). The average energy cost came to:[2]

— Wind energy	0.1-0.2 euro-cents/kWh
— Nuclear	0.4
— Hydro	0.4
— Coal	4.1-7.3
— Gas	1.3-2.3

Data about the US is equally revealing. As noted earlier, the capital costs of nuclear power are high although the operating and maintenance costs have become much lower than those for other sources of electricity. Volatility of fuel prices itself is a problem which is not really encountered in the case of nuclear power. Data concerning the US related to fuel plus operation and maintenance (O&M) costs (excluding capital costs) is plotted in Fig. 2. On the basis of the Organisation of Economic Cooperation and Development (OECD) projections, US costs for 2001 indicate a figure of 3.73 cents/kWh for nuclear energy, 3.27 cents/kWh for coal and 5.87 cents/kWh for gas.

Fig. 2. **US Electricity Production Costs**
(O & M+fuel) in constant 2001 cents/kWh

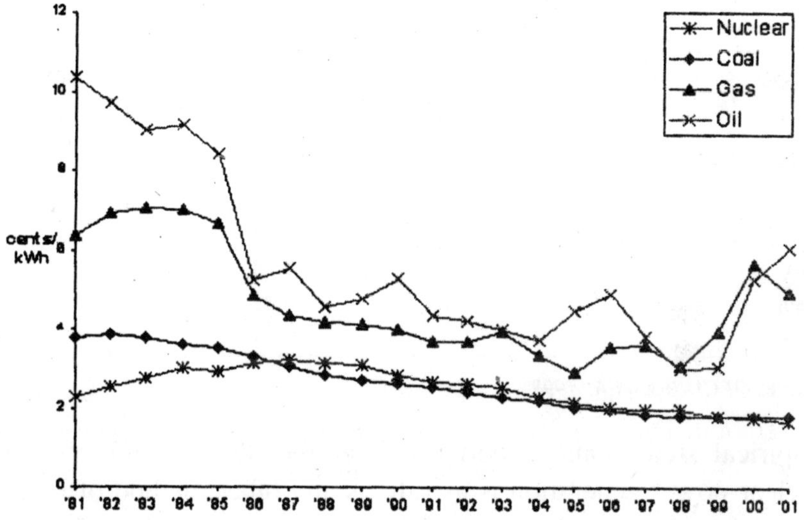

Source: US Utility Data Institute (pre-1995), Resource Data International (1995-)

French figures published in 2002 show the following costs:

— Nuclear energy	3.20 Euro-cents/kWh
— Gas	3.05 - 4.26
— Coal	3.81 - 4.57

The comparative electricity generation costs (at US 1997 constant cents per kWh of electricity) projections in various countries for the future covering the period 2005-10 based on studies by the OECD and International Energy Agency are indicated in Table 2.

Sustainable Energy for the Future

Concerns about the safety of nuclear power, which had shot up after the 1979 Three Mile Island accident and then by the one at Chernobyl in 1986 have long given way to greater understanding of the issues involved. Public perceptions and attitudes, however, are still deeply concerned about the safety factor even though all

Table 2. **Electricity Generation Cost Projections: 2005-2010**

(US 1997 cents/kWh)

	Nuclear	Coal	Gas
Canada	2.47-2.96	2.92	3.00
Russia	2.69	4.63	3.54
China	2.54-3.08	3.18	-
Korea	3.07	3.44	4.25
France	3.22	4.64	4.74
USA	3.33	2.48	2.33-2.71
Spain	4.10	4.22	4.79
Japan	5.75	5.58	7.91

Source: *OECD/IEA/NEA, 1998.*

empirical studies and experience over the decades indicate that nuclear power generation is as safe as any other method of power generation as long due care and precautions are taken. In fact, accumulation of experience and improvements in designs (especially with containment structures) and productivity have also improved the safety standards all across the world.

On the other hand, the environmental benefits of using nuclear power far exceed the negative effects of electricity generation by other methods. This is why, the then vice president of the United States and an ardent environmentalist, Al Gore, referring to the Chernobyl accident had stated that the lesson of the accident that destroyed the plant's unit number 4 "isn't an indictment of nuclear power as such. Nuclear power, designed well, regulated properly, and cared for meticulously, has a place in the world's energy supply."[3] This is obvious since nuclear power virtually does not emit any greenhouse gases. The complete nuclear power chain emits only 2-6 grams of carbon per kWh—that is, about the same as wind and solar power plants. If the world's 442 nuclear power plants were to shut down and be replaced with a proportionate mix of non-nuclear sources, the result would be an increase of 600 million tonnes of carbon per year which would be equal to the estimate of what can be avoided by the Kyoto Protocol in 2010.[4] The IAEA's relative estimates of greenhouse gas emissions from different sources of electricity generation are shown at Fig. 3.

Fig. 3. **Greenhouse Gas Emissions from Electricity Production**

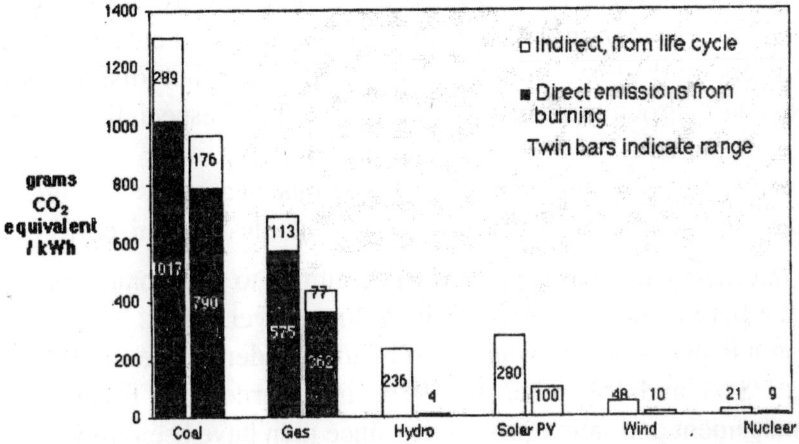

The environmental benefits of nuclear power are enormous indeed. But the issue of waste deserves note since this is a major concern. Nuclear energy produces both operational and decommissioning wastes which are contained and have been managed satisfactorily for over half a century. While there is no technical problem in dealing efficiently and safely with nuclear waste, the problem of nuclear waste is much more political and even ideological, focussing on final disposal. But nuclear power is the only energy-producing industry which takes full responsibility for all its waste and costs this into the product, thus, promoting sustainability.

There is no doubt that spent fuel from nuclear power reactors poses a very serious radioactive hazard although the volume of the spent fuel produced is not large. The scientific community is generally agreed that high-level waste and spent fuel can be disposed of safely. The entire nuclear industry in the United States produces approximately 2,000 tons of solid waste annually and elaborate arrangements have been made for its disposal. In comparison, coal-fired power generation utilities produce 100,000,000 tons of ash and sludge annually, laced in parts with poisons like mercury and nitric oxide. US industry itself generates 36,000,000 tons of hazardous waste which does not receive the care and attention that nuclear waste receives.[5] Oil spills are a major hazard in the world. The Exxon Valdez spill of 1989 was one of the worst environmental disasters in history, the scars of which have not disappeared. Pakistan's agricultural growth during 2003-04, especially in food production and fisheries (with a growth of a mere 2 per cent compared to 3.4 per cent in the previous year), has received a major setback because of the oil spill outside Karachi port.[6]

Nuclear safety has been, and will continue to be, a major concern in the field of nuclear reactors, including power plants. There have been numerous incidents and two major accidents, one in 1979 (in the USA) and the other in 1986 (in Chernobyl). Technology, management and safety procedures since then have been improving.

Notes

1. Donald C. Hitnz, president, Energy Corporation, and chairman, Nuclear Energy Institute, USA, in *Atoms for Peace: Nuclear Energy & Science for the Twenty-first Century* (Conference Report, USA, 2003).
2. "Nuclear Power's Changing Future," IAEA Press release, June 26, 2004, (http://www.iaea.org)
3. http://www.uic.com.au/nip08.htm
4. *Nuclear Energy Insight,* August 1998.
5. IAEA Press release, n. 2.
6. Nuclear Power: Energy for Today and Tomorrow, http:pw1.netcom.com/~res95/energy/nuclear.html
7. *Pakistan Economic Survey 2003-04,* Government of Pakistan, June 2004, ch. 2, p.11.

7

Inputs for a Nuclear Energy Policy for India

Manpreet Sethi

The need to meet the increasing energy requirements of a growing Indian population and a buoyant economy is one of the urgent concerns before the nation. Of all energy demands, that of reliable and affordable electricity is critical for the nation's economy and national security. Over the years, research and development of energy efficiency technologies, and an emphasis on renewable energy sources have been envisaged as being able to bridge the gap between electricity supply and demand. However, no substantive success in this endeavour is possible unless new generation capacities are added to meet the tremendous growth in demand. But the new electricity generation facilities must do so in an efficient, secure, cost-effective and safe manner that is also environmentally sustainable. All of these prerequisites are met by nuclear power and this calls for its acceptance as an important component in the country's energy mix.

Presently, 2720 MWe energy generated from 14 operational nuclear plants contributes about 3 per cent to the total energy generation in India. But this source of energy holds tremendous promise of expansion and can significantly contribute to the country's continued economic growth, its energy security and environmental health. Indeed, the relevance of nuclear power for

Dr. Manpreet Sethi is Senior Fellow, Centre for Strategic and International Studies, New Delhi.

the future must be understood today so that an adequate policy can be sagaciously drafted.

A nuclear energy policy for the future will have to not only be based on a realistic appraisal of what unique advantages nuclear power can offer to India, but also acknowledge the likely constraints on ambitious expansion plans and offer solutions to circumvent or surmount them. This paper examines the need for, and the limitations on, nuclear power in India, and suggests ways around them. With a view to aiding the formulation of a clear nuclear policy for the country, it concludes by offering certain constructive suggestions of both general and specific nature.

India's Need for Nuclear Power

A nuclear energy policy must first of all be grounded in the conviction that India has a rational and legitimate need for nuclear power. As brought out in the following sub-sections, many factors favour the growth of nuclear power in India and it would be foolhardy not to exploit them. Rather, it is imperative that this energy option is accorded due credit, and urgently.

Growing Energy Demand

Economic development and growth are the twin aspirations of an emergent India. But, among other factors, future economic growth will depend on the long-term availability of energy, particularly in the form of electricity. This will have to be available in increasing quantities and from sources that are stable, dependable, and low-cost. With the country fast emerging as a buoyant economy targeting an ambitious growth rate of seven to eight per cent over the next 20 years and with a growing population, an increase in India's energy consumption is certain.

According to World Bank estimates, energy demand in India will grow at 5.3 per cent per annum in the first decade of the 21st century and by 10 per cent by 2020. In case this demand is not met, the loss to India's economy, though difficult to quantify in figures, would be huge. Some estimates indicate that if the energy sector in India could reach international levels of performance, the country's Gross Domestic Product (GDP) would go up by an additional 2 per cent per annum.[1] Moreover, it is a fact that electricity today powers the nation's economic progress. As the economy becomes even more technology reliant in the coming years, electricity would play an even greater role as an economic multiplier. Increased availability of electricity would spur its wider and more diverse application. This, in turn, would lead to greater economic growth as the nation develops new ways to derive increased economic value from electricity and to improve overall standard of living. Therefore, increasing energy generation to meet growing demand is critical for continued economic growth and social development.

Limited Domestic Fuel Sources

Enhancing energy generation to the level required, however, cannot be possible only with domestic fuel sources. In the present Indian energy mix, coal[2] is the dominant fuel, meeting 55 per cent of primary energy consumption, with the share of oil at 36 per cent of total energy consumption.[3] Although India is rich in coal, only 20 per cent of the total coal transported to the power plants is of superior grade with ash content 24 per cent or less. The remaining 80 per cent is of an inferior grade with ash content ranging from 24 to 45 per cent. This coal, when used in thermal power plants, not only poses environmental problems, but also adversely affects plant performance, besides raising the cost of its operation and maintenance.[4] Hence, the need for import of high quality coal. In fact, there has been an increase in coal imports from 6 metric tonnes (MT) in 1991/92 to 20 MT in 1999/2000, a rate of growth of 16 per cent a year.[5]

Meanwhile, the country's hydrocarbon reserve is small at 0.4 per cent of the world's reserve. In fact, current reserve-to-production ratios for coal, oil and natural gas available in India are 235, 23 and 35 years respectively.[6] Already, India is a net importer of energy, with 20 per cent of its primary energy needs being met through imports. By 2030, India's demand for oil will increase to 36 per cent of total primary energy demand, requiring imports of almost 5 million barrels a day, unless there is a substantial increase in petroleum reserves. This will amount to an increase in India's import dependency for crude oil from 70 per cent in 1999-2000 to 90 per cent in the coming decades.[7] Natural gas is emerging as a replacement for oil, but if it is to be extensively used, it shall be necessary to import 70 per cent of this fuel too. Indian demand for natural gas is expected to grow by over 5 per cent per annum so as to meet 13 per cent of primary demand.[8] These figures are alarming not only because of the pressure they place on scarce foreign exchange resources but also because they pose a challenge to energy security.

Energy Security

For a country of India's size, dimension, population and economy, safeguarding energy is a strategic priority. This assumes even greater significance since India is yet a developing nation on the path of global ascendancy, but is grossly deficient in indigenous energy resources. Therefore, the challenge for India's national security in the coming decades is going to be to ensure a steady availability of energy. High dependence on energy imports raises security concerns ranging from the need to build elaborate and secure pipeline networks and other necessary infrastructure, to monitoring political and economic developments in countries/regions from where India sources the bulk of its imports. For a country with a large part of its one-billion-plus population without access to modern fuels, low overall income and consumption levels, and the urgency of accelerating economic growth, substantively increasing energy supply is a huge challenge. But nuclear power development holds a viable way out.

Environmental Concerns

When the bulk of the country's energy is sourced through fossil fuels (coal, oil and gas) that disperse CO_2 directly into the air, environmental consequences like greenhouse effect and global warming become a serious cause for concern. Thermal power plants pose the problem of greenhouse gas (GHG) emissions that cannot be wished away despite improvements in these technologies and stringent environmental measures applied at the plants. Rather, the pollution is sure to increase with the upsurge in energy production from thermal plants and would cause climate change and ozone depletion. In order to arrest these disturbing trends, environmental experts warn that the overall global CO_2 emissions should be cut from 25 billion tonnes annually to 10 billion tonnes, even as overall energy production increases.

Table 1 shows the CO_2 emissions from different energy sources in order to illustrate that coal, oil and gas remain major sources of carbon emissions, while nuclear and other renewable energy sources figure around the lowest.

Table 1. **Carbon Dioxide Emissions From Power Technologies in g/kWh**[9]

Coal	Advanced Coal	Oil	Gas	Nuclear	Biomass	PV	Hydro	Wind
960-1300	800-860	690-870	460-1230	9-100	37-166	30-150	2-410	11-75

At present, India's per capita energy consumption and hence, the resultant carbon emissions are relatively low. In 1997/98, the average per capita energy consumption of India was less than 0.5 tonnes of oil equivalent (TOE) compared to the world average of 1.7 TOE.[10] Consequently, in 1997, India emitted 250 kg of carbon per person, which was approximately one-quarter of the world average and less than 0.05 per cent of that in the US.[11] Despite these low figures, India is still the world's sixth largest CO_2 emitter.

This ranking would certainly change in the coming years for two reasons. One, because India would emerge as the world's most populated country by 2025 and its GHG emissions would rise consequently. Secondly, with energy demand projections what they are, if India continues to retain coal as the predominant fuel in its energy mix, the GHG emissions would certainly register a significant jump. It is estimated that India's total CO_2 emissions will rise from 0.9 billion tonnes to 2.3 billion tonnes by 2030, making it one of the largest carbon emitters.[12]

Given these estimates, the strategies and technologies India adopts to meet its energy demand will have critical implications for its own, and the global environment. Therefore, it is imperative that India is encouraged to adopt sustainable energy technologies that not only meet its future energy demand for rapid economic growth but also protect the environment. Surely, nuclear power technology merits consideration.

Economic Viability

It is an established fact that nuclear power is a genuine economic option in terms of long range marginal cost (LRMC) advantages for power supply at locations far away from coal reserves, particularly if hydel sources are also not available in these areas.[13] Of course, nuclear power plants are capital intensive with long gestation periods, but their operational and fuel costs are relatively much less and hence, the economics of nuclear power works out better. In fact, its cost-effectiveness is enhanced by the fact that India has successfully overcome the teething problems faced during indigenisation of the technology uptil the mid-1980s. Today, the country is one of the few that is entirely self-reliant. It has excellent research and development centres, a nuclear design set-up, engineering test labs, and a large construction and operating manpower. It has also mastered the complete fuel cycle from uranium mining and fuel fabrication to spent fuel reprocessing and radioactive waste disposal. In recent years, India's power plants have been running at good capacity utilisation levels. Plant load factors are now close to design levels, which means that operational costs are close to normative levels.[14]

Nuclear power's value as a carbon-free electricity supply technology would further be enhanced if and when in the future CO_2 emissions begin to carry a significant "price." While the possibility of this happening is still uncertain, given the ambiguity over the fate of Kyoto Protocol, sooner or later the need for carbon free sources of energy will be felt. In fact, it is noteworthy that even the MIT study conducted in the US on the "Future of Nuclear Power," recommends the retention of nuclear power, precisely because it is an important carbon-free source of power that can potentially make a significant contribution to future electricity supply and reducing GHG emissions.[15] Once a price is placed on emissions and emission trading gets under way, it would provide incentives for investment in carbon free electricity technologies, including nuclear power. In fact, then the economics of nuclear power would improve considerably since government policies that now focus on renewable energy resources and end-use efficiency improvements through a combination of direct subsidies, tax subsidies, and other mechanisms to promote carbon-free supply technologies would then have a stake in promoting nuclear power.

Vast Domestic Thorium Reserves

For India, the economics of nuclear power becomes more attractive because its long-term strategy envisages an exploitation of its vast thorium reserves. The Indian nuclear power programme was formulated along three stages linking the fuel cycles of a pressurised heavy water reactor (PHWR) to a fast breeder reactor (FBR) with the use of thorium eventually in the advanced heavy water reactor (AHWR). This strategy was devised for the judicious use of our limited uranium ore, estimated to be at 78,000 tonnes or 0.8 per cent of the world resources, and the vast thorium reserves at 360,000 tonnes. It was realised quite early on in the country's nuclear planning that domestic uranium reserves could not contribute significantly to the energy scenario if used on a once-through basis and then disposed off as waste. It was, therefore, devised that the plutonium produced in PHWRs would be used in FBRs along with thorium to produce additional nuclear fuel. In the third stage, thorium and U-233 based nuclear reactors are expected to meet the long-term energy requirements of India.

Constraints on Indian Nuclear Power Expansion

Based on all of the above factors, it can be concluded that nuclear power does have certain inherently unique advantages for India. Therefore, it makes eminent sense to not only keep the option of nuclear power expansion open, but to press for it urgently. However, there are certain limiting factors that must be taken into account.

Financing

At present, nuclear plant construction is on the fast track and money does not appear to be as serious a problem as it once was, but it cannot be forgotten that traditionally, lack of adequate financing has been an important constraint on nuclear power expansion. Insufficient budgetary allocations for a capital-intensive nuclear power programme plagued this source of energy since it was not thought to be cost-competitive. Delays caused as a consequence of inadequate funds made the projects even more expensive than they needed to be and further contributed to the perception. Long gestation periods and increasing legislative requirements on safety regulations also made the plants unattractive for private investors.

For India, this problem was further magnified because, unlike other countries where development of the nuclear power sector could occur with the help of international cooperation supported by funding credit, this advantage was denied to India. It was blocked from receiving equity participation or loans from foreign sources because technology control regimes did not permit such assistance unless India accepted fullscope safeguards. Therefore, so far, nuclear power in India has solely been owned and funded by the government, with only limited financing from the public in the form of short-term maturity bonds. Hence, lack of adequate financial resources hampered the pace of development of India's nuclear programme, particularly through the 1980s and 1990s. This was also the time when the indigenously built nuclear plants were suffering from technical snags. Delays in construction and shutdowns were frequent, adding to the costs of nuclear power.

More recently, however, nuclear plants have established their economic viability. The Nuclear Power Corporation of India Ltd. (NPCIL), a public sector undertaking of the Department of Atomic Energy (DAE) that is tasked with the designing, construction and operation of nuclear power reactors has significantly improved the performance of nuclear plants and accumulated 200 reactor years of nuclear power plant operation. The average capacity factor of the plants has touched more than 80 per cent in most cases, and finances are no longer the problem as earlier.

However, if nuclear power is to play a larger role in future Indian energy generation, it would be necessary to explore newer options of augmenting and diversifying financial investments. In a comparative, market oriented environment, even the government will be compelled to justify every paisa of investment and unless nuclear power continues to maintain and enhance its economic edge, it might find government funding receding in favour of other energy sources. It is for this reason that the Department of Atomic Energy (DAE) chairman, in a talk delivered at the First National Conference on Nuclear Reactor Safety, emphasised the importance of cost rationalisation at every level of the nuclear programme. He underlined the need to prove the commercial viability of every stage of the programme and gave equal credence to safety, technology and profitability as factors that would determine the flow of investments for its future development.

Technology Denial Regimes

On account of its non-acceptance of the nuclear Non-Proliferation Treaty (NPT) and fullscope safeguards (FSS) as applied under the International Atomic Energy Agency (IAEA) safeguards regime, the Zangger Committee and the Nuclear Suppliers Group ((NSG) guidelines have denied India nuclear and dual-use technology, materials, and knowhow. Both these seek to control all nuclear trade through an elaborate safeguards system in order to minimise the risk of imported nuclear materials and technology being hijacked for weapons development. In the bargain, however, export controls have often fettered the development of peaceful power programmes. India has particularly felt this disadvantage because in the absence of access to advanced nuclear technology and materials unless it accepts FSS, the country's nuclear power sector has suffered cost overruns and time delays.

India has responded to these denial regimes by indigenising the nuclear processes, materials and technology. While it has achieved a high level of self-reliance that shall sustain the power programme, if India is to urgently add nuclear power to its total energy generation capacities, it would greatly help if technological, material and financial support were to become available from outside. In fact, for the requisite growth of nuclear energy in India, it would be important that the country be assured of:

(a) security of supply of nuclear materials and components;
(b) access to more efficient and newer reactor technologies;
(c) simpler and easier arrangements on importing nuclear reactors, materials and components.

Continued Availability of Uranium at Low Cost

More than any of the above constraints, the rapid expansion of the nuclear power programme could be hampered in the future by the shortage of uranium. Since 1968, the Uranium Corporation of India Ltd, (UCIL) has been commercially producing and processing uranium ore mainly from the mines at Jaduguda, Bhatin, Narwapahar and Turamdih, all located in Singhbhum district of Jharkhand. This has been sufficient for the operating power plants and research reactors. However, over the decades, the uranium reserves have depleted and the ore at Jaduguda mines is presently being obtained at much deeper levels than earlier. This pushes up the cost of recovery of uranium, which in the case of India is in any case high because of low concentration of uranium in the ore. Indian ore has uranium content as low as 0.6 per cent and, hence, the price of uranium for India is much higher than in the international market. But uranium is not available to India from the open international market because of the NSG guidelines.

To meet the projected demand of the nuclear power programme, UCIL is planning the exploration of uranium deposits located in other areas of Jharkhand and in Andhra Pradesh and Meghalaya. Its efforts in this direction, however, have been mired in controversy since local populace and non-governmental activities in the regions have opposed all such attempts. Lack of availability of uranium for a programme that moves from 10,000-15,000 MWe to a few 100,000 MWe would pose a major constraint. Also, high costs of recovery would be adversely reflected in the unit energy cost.

Limitations of Indian Manufacturing Industry

Given the sensitive nature of materials involved and the high technology content of nuclear power, it is imperative that the Indian manufacturing industry keeps pace with the advancing nuclear science and technology and provides it with the necessary infrastructure and equipment. For instance, the nuclear plants require precision equipment of particular specifications, robotics equipment, huge pressure vessels of special metals, etc., materials and equipment that may have little commercial value since they are not used by many other industries. However, in view of the fact that the same are not available to India from outside sources because of NSG restrictions, the Indian nuclear industry has to depend only upon the domestic industry and its capabilities. This may sometimes call for the redesigning of components or reformulation of specifications to match available standards.

Public Perception of Nuclear Energy

Yet another significant obstacle to rapid and large-scale nuclear power expansion is public perception of this source as one that poses danger to human health, and to the environment. The Three

Mile Island incident and Chernobyl have been publicised enough to create opposition to nuclear power. Unfortunately, there is very little awareness of the stringent safety regulations enforced and followed in the design, construction and operation of power plants, or of the safety record of India's power plants of nearly three and a half decades. Neither is there adequate knowledge of the fact that natural radiation in some cases exists several times more than in the vicinity of a power plant.

Suggestions for Policy-Making

In the light of the above issues, the following section offers certain suggestions that can help in the making of a nuclear energy policy for India. First of all, it is necessary that at the government level, a place of prominence is accorded to nuclear energy as a vital component of the national energy and environmental policy. This will then be reflected in the funding available for various development tasks in the field of nuclear power technology. Further suggestions are clubbed under two heads—general and specific.

General Suggestions

- *Get the NSG to Apply a Country Specific Approach to India*

Nuclear imports into India are presently possible only in the case of two eventualities: one, if India were to accept FSS under the IAEA safeguards regime; and second, if the NSG guidelines were to be suitably amended or ignored. The possibility of either of these appears extremely remote. But there may be a third compromise scenario and that is if the NSG guidelines were to treat India as a unique case that merits certain country-specific concessions. In order to press for this, it is imperative that the NSG countries are made to comprehend the issues that make India an exceptional case. *India is going to be the energy demand heartland of the world in the coming decades. Its ability to meet this demand will have huge consequences for the economy of the world. But even more significant, how it meets this demand will spell equally huge consequences for the global environment. Hence, making nuclear power technology and materials available to India would be in the larger and long-term interests of the international community.*

Secondly, the uniqueness of India's position stems from its *de facto* status as a nuclear weapon state (NWS). While the dominant powers led by the United States do not wish to acknowledge India as an NWS, leave alone accord it a *de jure* status, they are increasingly aware of the reality that India is a *de facto* NWS and shall exist so until universal nuclear disarmament becomes a reality. As far as the NSG is concerned, it does not specifically define a nuclear or non-nuclear state in its guidelines. Nevertheless, the guidelines are applied in a selective manner since FSS do not apply in the case of NWS. Also, one interpretation of INFCIRC/254, Part 1 establishes that NWS are not subject to the requirement of final use guarantees.[16] Therefore, the question is whether the NSG can take the *de facto* status/capabilities of India into account and, hence, treat it differently from others. In fact, if India were to be accepted as a country at par with the NWS for the limited purpose of requisite waivers/concessions in the NSG guidelines, then it would not have to accept FSS. Russian diplomats have already argued that since India has become a *de facto* NWS, looser controls should be applied over nuclear exports that should be allowed to it.[17]

Another factor that must be highlighted is that India's nuclear exports have always been for peaceful purposes, above board, and subject to IAEA requirements. This quality of India is particularly relevant in the contemporary scenario when revelations about nuclear proliferation through a thriving black market have shaken the existing non-proliferation regime. In contrast, India's record as a nuclear exporter is commendable. It has a stringent export policy in place and no likelihood of imports finding their way into the wrong hands. To further illustrate the point, Table 2 graphically details the proliferation behaviour of five countries.

Table 2. **Comparative Proliferation Behaviour**

Criterion	USA	Russia	China	India	Pakistan
Use of nuclear weapons	Yes	No	No	No	No
Deployed missile based nuclear forces in territories of other countries	Yes	Yes	Yes	No	No
Provided another country with weapons design, information, test data or computer codes hardware or special nuclear material	Yes	Yes	Yes	No	Yes
Received nuclear weapons design information, test data, hardware or special nuclear material	No	No	Yes	No	Yes
Supplied nuclear assistance to unsafeguarded facility	Yes	Yes	Yes	No	Yes
Violated non-proliferation commitments	Yes	Yes	Yes	No	Yes

As is clearly evident, India is the only country that despite not being bound by any formal commitment to the non-proliferation regimes and export guidelines has still abided by them most diligently. *Given this track record and its domestic export control legislative infrastructure, there is no reason why the NSG members should not accord it a special consideration for the supply of nuclear exports.*

- *Exploit NSG-Related Possibilities*

NSG guidelines do not have the force or sanctity of an international treaty as each NSG member, through requisite national legislation, implements these voluntarily. While the guidelines are adopted through consensus, they do no more than offer a set of principles that supplier nations must apply while processing applications for exports. But the actual decision on the application is taken at the national level in accordance with national export licensing requirements. This largely voluntary nature of the NSG guidelines, applied at the national level, at the discretion of the national legislature, allows some room for interpretation, and national laws, if so desired, can be tailored or amended to allow for nuclear exports.

Secondly, NSG guidelines *permit islanded safeguards* or transfer of nuclear technology without FSS under two special circumstances:

(a) In the case of transfers that pertain to agreements or contracts drawn up on, or prior to, April 3, 1992. It is on this ground that the Indo-Russian Koodankulam agreement has been justified.

(b) In exceptional cases when such transfers are essential for the safe operation of existing facilities and on humanitarian grounds. Interestingly, the NSG guidelines do not define the exceptional cases when safety considerations apply. But the *safety clause* has been used and can be invoked by countries desirous of exporting nuclear technologies to India.

- *Make Use of Improving Indo-US Relations*

The thaw in bilateral relations of the two largest democracies has seen the emergence of a strategic relationship, including cooperation in areas of high technology such as space and nuclear. After his visit to the US in December 2003, then Indian Prime Minister Atal Behari Vajpayee said that a "groundbreaking nuclear and high-tech pact with the United States was a milestone in bilateral ties." US President George W. Bush too promised closer links with India over nuclear regulation and safety, missile defence and civilian use of space technology.[18] The agreement between the two has shifted requests for export of sensitive technologies to India from "presumption of denial" to "presumption of approval."[19]

Some Indian analysts, however, are still sceptional that the constructive engagement with the US would result in Washington going to the extent of amending or circumventing NSG guidelines to help India's power programme.[20] Nevertheless, the "glide path" does hold a lot of promise. Most importantly, the initiative implies an attempt by the US to find ways of cooperating in areas that were hitherto regarded as taboo. It is most certain to result in American assistance in safety mechanisms for India's nuclear facilities, as well as greater cooperation between the nuclear regulatory agencies of the two countries. In a broader sense, it will ease unilateral licensing requirements for the transfer of high technology and dual-use items.

These developments are not of little significance. For one, they would enhance nuclear safety in India, foster a better bilateral understanding between the nuclear establishments and pave the way for greater cooperation in the future. Secondly, at another level, the initiation of US contribution to India's nuclear power programme would encourage other keen nuclear suppliers, such as France and Russia, to bid deals for their nuclear industries as well.

Specific Suggestions

For the sake of clarity and coherence, the specific suggestions may be divided into three categories:

Related to Nuclear Industry

- Simplify and standardise the designs of nuclear reactors in order to reduce system complexities, enhance operator-friendliness, easy maintainability and thereby reduce costs and increase operational efficiency.
- Build a larger number of successive units with one time commitment and standardised design to reduce manufacturing cycles, manufacturing costs and overall project costs.
- Reduce the gestation period for nuclear power projects through improved planning ahead of construction and by streamlining clearances from AERB, MOFE, Pollution Control Board, etc.
- Match power plant expansion with simultaneous augmentation of other fuel cycle facilities.
- Explore the possibility of joint sector projects and private sector participation to mobilise additional financial resources.

- Encourage international and regional cooperation in the field of nuclear power. The global need for improvements in plant safety standards and global environmental concerns demand this. The sharing of experience and information would be a *win-win* situation for all, particularly in the areas of research and development, design standardisation, management competence, training, safety, environment and regulatory practices.
- Seek participation in international innovative projects as a member of IAEA and, thus, enhance the national knowledge base.
- Undertake safety enhancement to maintain the excellent record so that safe and reliable operation of plants overseen by a consistent and stringent regulatory process would enhance support for nuclear power.
- Implement safe and wise spent fuel and radioactive waste management that can envisage solutions for the issue before it becomes too big, including finding suitable repository sites.
- Maintain high level of scientific research and its synergy with technology.

Related to Other Industries

- Encourage industries, through subsidies or tax benefits, to develop the necessary infrastructure and qualified human resources to meet the high technology needs of the nuclear industry.
- Build a large number of successive units so that the industry is guaranteed consistent orders that justify its capacity and resources dedicated to meeting nuclear industry requirements.
- Expand interface between the Bhabha Atomic Research Centre (BARC) and universities and other industries to reap benefits of collaborative research and development.

- Encourage universities to place emphasis on basic research in nuclear sciences and allied areas, including in condensed matter physics, high energy physics, molecular and optic sciences, laser chemistry, interfacial chemistry, etc.

Related to Uranium Availability

- Research and development of techniques to recover uranium from secondary sources.
- Speed up the second stage of India's nuclear power programme that would demonstrate FBRs as a commercially viable venture.
- Work on development of fast reactor fuel cycle, including establishment of plants for reprocessing and refabrication of fuel for fast reactors.
- Move rapidly to Stage III of the power programme to undertake technology demonstration for large-scale thorium utilisation.

Related to Public Awareness

- Spread better appreciation of importance of clean and plentiful electricity for social and economic development.
- Increase public awareness about the excellent safety ratings of nuclear plants worldwide, and in India.
- Increase transparency of issues related to nuclear waste management and highlight that nuclear energy produces less than 1.2 per cent of waste by weight than the best competing fuel, natural gas.
- Enhance public understanding of nuclear power and radiation science to increase public demand for nuclear energy.
- Spread awareness of the overwhelming benefits of radiation technology in areas of societal relevance such as health care, agriculture, food preservation, water desalination, etc.

- Publicise high standards of physical security of Indian plants and the unlikelihood of proliferation therefrom.

Conclusion

Nuclear technology in India has reached a state of self-reliance. The existing power plants are working well and have achieved high and international level capacity factors. The Indian nuclear power programme has also moved into the second stage of development wherein a prototype FBR is now under construction, and research and development for AHWRs is under way.

It should be pointed out at this juncture that the Indian nuclear power programme is charting its own unique course, not treaded by another country so far. In fact, it is quite contrary to the path recommended to the US nuclear programme by the MIT Study on the Future of Nuclear Power in the US. This had recommended: "For the next decades, government and industry in the United States and elsewhere should give priority to deployment of the once-through fuel cycle, rather than development of the more expensive closed fuel cycle technology involving reprocessing and new advanced thermal or fast reactor technologies." For the US, the open, once-through fuel cycle is believed to best meet the criteria of economic attractiveness and proliferation resistance. But India's realities and priorities are different.

Given India's constraints of uranium, it does not have the luxury of following the cheaper open fuel cycle wherein the spent fuel discharged from the reactor may be discarded as waste. Instead, India must follow the closed fuel cycle that envisages the reprocessing of spent fuel discharged from the reactor so that it may be partitioned into uranium (U) and plutonium (Pu) suitable for fabrication into oxide fuel or mixed oxide fuel (MOX) for recycle back into a reactor. Uranium shortage compels reprocessing and the pursuit of fast breeder reactor technology in order to use the vast thorium deposits at a later state in an AHWR. The Indian uranium reserves, at about 0.8 per cent of the world, cannot sustain a large nuclear power programme if it is used on once-through basis. Rather, in a carefully planned programme, the available uranium is to be used to harness the energy contained in non-fissile thorium, of which India possesses about 32 per cent of the world's reserves. Therefore, given India's unique concerns, and for its long-term energy security, it has no option but to deploy nuclear power according to a strategy precisely tuned to its needs and resources.

Hence, despite the costs, and even as it bears the brunt of technology denial, India must press ahead with its nuclear power programme to the extent, and at the pace possible. Of course, import of nuclear material,knowhow and technology would give a fillip and speed to the programme. As this paper has argued, this may be possible in certain situations and it is imperative that the nuclear energy policy suitable reflects these. It must be highlighted at every level and forum that the country's buoyant economy demands energy. And the increasing environmental problems demand that this energy be generated in a manner that is environmentally sustainable. Of course, economics is an important consideration for harnessing any energy source, but one may recall Dr. Bhabha's remark made four decades ago, "No power is costlier than no power." Indeed, lack of power could impose a severe economic penalty on the country and prove more costly than the costliest of energy generation technologies. Nuclear power offers many advantages to India. A comprehensive policy on its expansion must be urgently drafted and implemented if India is not to let unavailability of power stand in the way of its economic growth and development.

Notes

1. R.K. Pachauri, "Defining an Integrated Energy Strategy for India," TERI website at http://www.teriin.org/energy/
2. According to British Petroleum estimates, Indian coal reserves comprise eight per cent of the world total. The country is the fourth largest producer of coal and lignite in the world (after the United States, China, and Australia). Despite India's large reserves of coal, there has been an increase in coal imports, which have grown from 6 MT in 1991/92 to 20 MT in 1999/2000, a rate of growth of 16 per cent a year (MoC 2001). TERI, n. 1.

3. India's import dependency for crude oil is likely to increase from 70 per cent in the 1999-2000 to 90 per cent in the coming decades. See Jasjit Singh, ed., *Oil and Gas in India's Security* (New Delhi: Knowledge World, July 2000. p. ix.
4. Sajal Ghosh, "Sustainable Energy Policies for Clean Air in India," *Background Paper* prepared for The Atlantic Council, USA, p. 9.
5. Ministry of Commerce, Annual Report (New Delhi: Ministry of Commerce, 2001).
6. Ghosh, n. 4, p. 9.
7. Singh, ed., n. 3, p. ix.
8. Asia clean air.
9. Rangan Bannerjee, "Assessment of Role of Renewable Energy Technologies," Greenhouse Gas Pollution Prevention Project—Climate Change Supplement, The Louis Berger Group Inc. Global Environment Team available at http://www.climachangeindia.com/gep/ccs/.
10. Amit Kumar, "Energy Scenario in South Asia," *Energy Technology News* (TERI), Issue 1, October 2000.
11. Ibid.
12. Asia clean air.
13. Yoginder K. Alagh, "Economics of Nuclear Power in India," *Nu-Power International,* vol. 11, no. 1-3, 1997, p. 22.
14. The Candu Owners Group declared India's operating PHWRs the world's best performing plants for the period 1999-2002. The gross capacity factor of these plants was 90 per cent, even ahead of the USA. Kakrapar I was adjudged the world's best performer in 2003. *Nu-Power,* vol. 17, no. 1-3, 2003.
15. MIT, *The Future of Nuclear Power* (Massachusetts: MIT, 2003).
16. Point made by Carmen Richter Ribeiro Moura, Division of Disarmament and Sensitive Technologies, Ministry of External Relations, Brazil, at the NSG organised International Seminar on the "Role of Export Controls in Nuclear Non-Proliferation," Vienna, October 7-8, 1997.
17. WISE (Amsterdam) News Communique, "India: Construction of Koodankulam Begins," October 19, 2001.
18. "India Says Deeper Nuclear Ties With US Mark Key Milestone in Ties," *Agence France Press,* January 13, 2004.
19. Jyoti Malhotra, "Out of Pokharan Shadow, India, US to Sign Hi-Tech Deal," *Indian Express,* December 19, 2003.
20. J.N. Dixit, "This Subcontinental Shift," *Indian Express* (Delhi), February 23, 2004.

